MEGA REX

A TYRANNOSAURUS NAMED SCOTTY

Dr. W. Scott Persons IV

with illustrations by Beth Zaiken

HARBOUR PUBLISHING

Page 1: Taller than a giraffe and heavier than an elephant, Scotty the *T. rex* was one big beast.

Pages 2–3: A young *Tyrannosaurus rex* walks through the forest. Not yet a giant, the dinosaur is on the hunt for small prey and on the lookout for larger predators.

Harbour Publishing Co. Ltd.
P.O. Box 219, Madeira Park, BC, V0N 2H0
www.harbourpublishing.com

Photos by Royal Saskatchewan Museum except: page 54 reprinted from *The American Museum Journal* 16, no. 1 (1919): frontispiece; page 81 by arul_nkh / Shutterstock; page 39 (bottom) courtesy Blue Rhino Studio; page 97 by Holly Cheyenne; page 71 (top) courtesy Karen Chin; pages 45, 78 (top) courtesy Phil Currie; page 73 (top) courtesy Robert DePalma; page 43 courtesy Greg Erickson; page 32 by Michael Gray / Flickr; pages 6 (top left), 7 (top), 12–13, 14, 15, 16 (bottom), 20 (all), 29 (bottom), 47, 58–59, 63, 64, 72, 80 (Specimen in the Collections of the Royal Tyrell Museum of Palaeontology), 82, 83 (all), 86, 90 (bottom), 91, 95, 96, 115, 117 by Amanda Kelley; page 55 reprinted from W.D. Matthew, *Dinosaurs with Special Reference to the American Museum Collections*, American Museum of Natural History (New York, 1915); pages 66, 67 courtesy Ariana Paulina; pages 36 (bottom), 87 (all) by Scott Persons; page 31 by Stephen Rahn / Flickr; page 36 (top) courtesy Jon Runolfson; page 74 (top) courtesy Eric Snively; page 39 (top) courtesy Beth Zaiken.

Illustrations on page 6 (map of North America) by ad_hominem / Adobe Stock; pages 112–13 by Daniel / Adobe Stock; page 91 by dottedyeti / Adobe Stock; pages 110–11 by Mohamad Haghani / Alamy Stock Photo; pages 104–5 by Mohamad Haghani / Stocktrek Images / Alamy Stock Photo; page 92 by Herschel Hoffmeyer / Shutterstock.com; page 56 by Ralf Juergen Kraft / Shutterstock.com; page 109 by Sergey Krasovskiy / Stocktrek Images / Alamy

Stock Photo; page 116 by Naz-3D / Shutterstock. com; pages 30 (based on an illustration by Peter Larson), 48 (bottom), 49, 50–51, 53, 57 (based on an illustration by Scott Hartman), 59 (based on an illustration by Scott Hartman), 60–61 (all), 68–69 (based on an illustration by Ashley Morhardt), 70 (based on an illustration by Scott Hartman), 80, 88–89 (bottom, top right), 101 (all), 108, 117 (based on an image by Victoria Arbour), 118 (bottom) by Nathan Rogers; page 100 by Emily Willoughby / Stocktrek Images / Alamy Stock Photo.

Edited and indexed by Brianna Cerkiewicz
Cover design by Diane Robertson
Text typeset by Roger Handling and Sari Naworynski
Printed and bound in Canada
Printed on Forest Stewardship Council–certified paper

Canadä

Canada Council for the Arts   Conseil des Arts du Canada

BRITISH COLUMBIA ARTS COUNCIL   BRITISH COLUMBIA

Harbour Publishing acknowledges the support of the Canada Council for the Arts, the Government of Canada, and the Province of British Columbia through the BC Arts Council.

Library and Archives Canada Cataloguing in Publication

Title: Mega rex : a tyrannosaurus named Scotty / Dr. W. Scott Persons IV with illustrations by Beth Zaiken.
Names: Persons, W. Scott, IV, author. | Zaiken, Beth, illustrator.
Description: Includes index.
Identifiers: Canadiana (print) 20200195174 | Canadiana (ebook) 20200195166 | ISBN 9781550179057 (softcover) | ISBN 9781550179064 (HTML)
Subjects: LCSH: Tyrannosaurus rex—Saskatchewan—Juvenile literature. | LCSH: Tyrannosaurus rex—Juvenile literature.
Classification: LCC QE862.S3 P47 2020 | DDC j567.912/9—dc23)

To my two greatest teachers:
Dr. Robert Bakker, who helped me find my first dinosaur and
Dr. Phil Currie, who took me into his office one day and said he had a new research project for me. He said it was a *T. rex*, and he said it was big.

CONTENTS

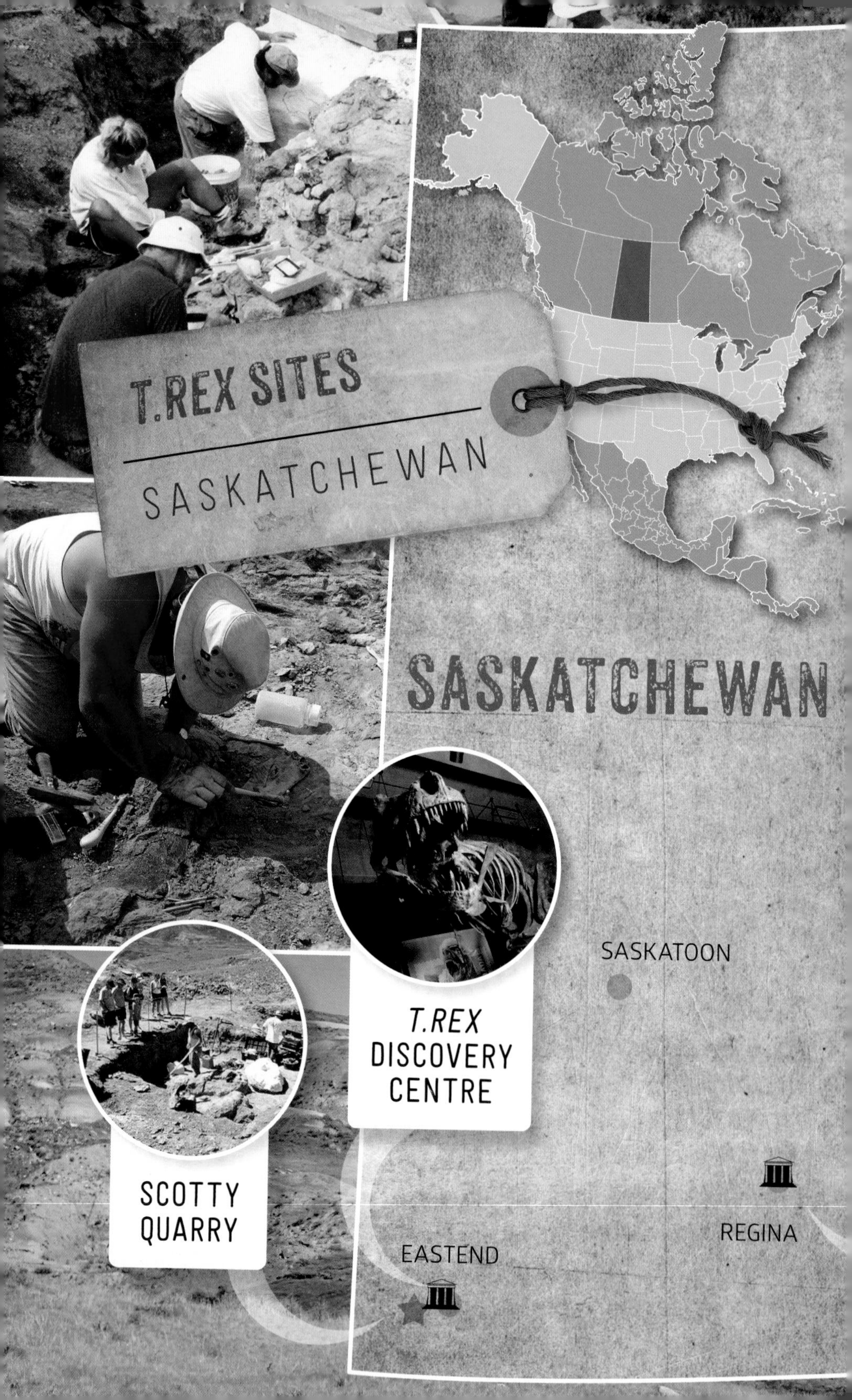

T.REX SITES
SASKATCHEWAN

SASKATCHEWAN

T.REX
DISCOVERY
CENTRE

SASKATOON

SCOTTY
QUARRY

EASTEND

REGINA

ROYAL SASKATCHEWAN MUSEUM

IT'S 66 MILLION YEARS AGO ...

And you're hungry. The sun is starting to set, and one of your favourite foods is now out and about. You're an *Acheroraptor*, a kind of raptor dinosaur. You're on the hunt for the little **mammal** *Alphadon*. These fuzzy creatures are no bigger than your feathery head, and they're delicious. You sniff and your nose breathes in the prehistoric air. It's warm and smells of salt from the sea, which is only a few kilometres away.

Part of you wants to give up on this hunt. You're in a dangerous corner of the forest. You know that a terrible beast lives here. Another part of you thinks that you just need to stay quiet. The hunt might only take a little longer, and then you won't be hungry anymore. You take another sniff. You can smell your prey. You bend down over a hollow log and sniff again. Yes! There's an *Alphadon* hiding inside. You focus all your attention on the log. How far in can your jaws reach?

CRACK

This *Acheroraptor* knows there is a delicious little mammal hiding in that log. But in the Age of Dinosaurs, a predator can quickly become prey.

Behind you, a branch breaks. You turn around and forget all about your hunger. Looking down at you is a *Tyrannosaurus rex*! The *T. rex* is big, nearly three times as long as you and ten times as heavy. It lunges forward, and you run as fast as you can. The *T. rex* snaps at your tail and yanks out three of your tail feathers. Those feathers will grow back, but that was too close! As a raptor, you're fast. But the *T. rex* is just as quick. You can't outrun it. You need to go up. Like your tail, your arms have large feathers, but you can't fly. What you *can* do is climb. You leap onto the trunk of a tall tree. The *T. rex* turns just a little too slowly. You climb up and out onto a high branch.

CHOMP *CHOMP*

The *T. rex* snaps its jaws below you. It can chomp all it wants. You're too high up. You look down and hiss at the *T. rex*. Angry, the *T. rex* snaps its jaws again and lets out a loud grunt. That ... was a mistake. A different grunt, this one louder and deeper, sounds through the forest. Now, it's the *T. rex*'s turn to look back and be afraid.

The scariest dinosaur that your raptor eyes have ever seen steps out of the trees. Mist swirls around its feet. This is the beast that you knew lurked in the forest. It's another *Tyrannosaurus rex*, but this one is very old and fully grown. It's twice the size of the *T. rex* that chased you. It walks forward and lets out another grunt. The first *T. rex* is clearly terrified. It shrinks back, then turns and runs even faster than when it was chasing you.

An *Acheroraptor* and *T. rex* size each other up. When you have long arms and strong claws, a tree makes for a good hiding place. But to avoid the reach of a full-grown *T. rex*, you had better be sure it's a very tall tree.

The huge *Tyrannosaurus rex* advances. You can tell it doesn't want to eat the other *T. rex*. It has a full belly and must have just had a large meal. But it does want to make sure the other *T. rex* knows whose territory this is and that intruders had better stay out. As the giant walks towards your tree, you decide to climb up a few branches higher.

Your Guide

Hi! My name is Dr. Scott Persons. I'm a **paleontologist**, a scientist who studies **fossils** and prehistoric life. One of the coolest fossils I have ever studied is the enormous skeleton

of a *Tyrannosaurus rex* nicknamed "Scotty." No, Scotty isn't named after me, but I am the paleontologist who led the first scientific study of Scotty. Our research team discovered that Scotty is an unusual *Tyrannosaurus rex*. Scotty quickly became a famous dinosaur. Newspapers and television reporters wanted to film and photograph the skeleton, and speak with paleontologists about its discovery. Why? Mostly because Scotty is big—so big that it has been called the "Mega Rex."

But there's much more to Scotty than just its size. Figuring it out took careful research by many paleontologists. Thanks to all their scientific work, the "Mega Rex" has taught us how a *Tyrannosaurus rex* lived, hunted, fought, survived and grew from the size of a house cat to the size of a school bus. Let me tell you the story of Scotty.

Scotty the *T. rex* has been dead for over 65 million years, but staring headlong into its jaws is still intimidating.

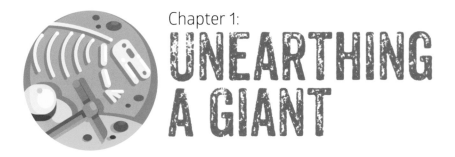

Chapter 1

UNEARTHING A GIANT

Pieces of the Past

The bones of Scotty the *Tyrannosaurus rex*, or of any other kind of dinosaur, are one type of fossil. A fossil is any object from the past that tells us about prehistoric life. Usually, a fossil is a piece of the body of a prehistoric animal, plant or other kind of living thing. So, we call such fossils **body fossils**. After death, most living things rot away. But some kinds of life (including you and I) have body parts that are made of hard, durable material. Teeth, bones and the shells of many animals don't easily rot. Still, they'll eventually crumble apart

A chunk of petrified wood (right), a prehistoric seashell (top left) and an ancient crocodile tooth are all body fossils.

if they remain lying exposed on the ground. However, if they get buried in sand or mud and that sand or mud eventually hardens into stone, then those hard body parts can be preserved as fossils. Fossils can last for many millions of years. While the fossil is buried, water that is slowly seeping through the ground may bring tiny bits of dirt and rock inside very small openings in the body fossil. These bits of dirt and rock will eventually fill all the empty spaces inside of a fossil. This filling can get cemented together and make the fossil as hard as the rock it's buried in (sometimes harder). It's rare, but even if a body part is soft, like a feather, fingernail or scale, it can also fossilize if it gets buried really quickly.

Not all fossils are body parts. Some are **trace fossils**. Trace fossils record the actions of a living thing. Fossil footprints, burrows and nests are all examples of trace fossils. It's possible for a fossil to be both a body fossil and a trace fossil. Have a look at this piece of rib from an **herbivorous** dinosaur. A rib is part of the skeleton, so this is clearly a body fossil. Look closely and you will see the rib has scratch marks on it. Those scratch marks were left by the tooth of a **carnivorous** dinosaur as it was munching on the rib. The scratches record the action of eating, so this is also a trace fossil.

Two fossils in one! The scratches on this piece of dinosaur bone were left by another dinosaur's bite.

TEAM REX:
Robert Gebhardt
A Bone in the Badlands

Robert Gebhardt is a school teacher who lives in the small town of Eastend, Saskatchewan. He's always been fascinated by prehistoric animals. Robert loves hunting for fossils in the **badlands** around his home, and he's really good at it. In the summer of 1991, Robert was asked by the Royal Saskatchewan Museum if he would like to join them on an expedition. Robert said, "Yes."

The expedition was going well. The team had found lots of small fossils, including the bony backplates of a prehistoric crocodile, the tail and toe bones of several duck-billed dinosaurs and many teeth that probably belonged to a *Triceratops*. But no one had found anything really great and the hiking wasn't easy. It was hot, and the slopes of the badlands were steep. Still, Robert hiked on. He came to a

Scotty was found tail first. This is one of Scotty's broken tail bones. The brown part is the real fossil. The white part is putty, which is used to fill in the gaps and hold the bone together.

Returning to the site many years later, Robert Gebhardt shows where his big discovery was made.

small canyon where he'd never stopped to look for fossils before. As he hiked down the slope, he spotted something sticking out of the ground. Robert bent down and pulled a brush and small pick from his backpack. As he scraped and swept around the fossil, he realized it was something interesting. The fossil looked big, and as he dug, it kept looking bigger. It was so large that it had to be from a dinosaur. Robert stood up and yelled to his teammates, who were spread out across the badlands.

Paleontologists Tim Tokaryk and Dr. John Storer sprinted over. From one look, they could tell the bone wasn't from a duckbill or a *Triceratops*. The bones of most big herbivorous (plant-eating) dinosaurs have an outer surface that looks a bit like wood. On the inside, the bones are spongy, with only a small hollow space. The bone that Robert had found wasn't like that. It was smooth and shiny on the outside and looked like porcelain. Where the bone was broken open, they could see it had thin walls with a big hollow space on the inside. Bones with thin walls and lots of hollow space usually belong to carnivorous (meat-eating) dinosaurs. No one knew it at the time, but Robert had just discovered the biggest dinosaur skeleton ever found in Canada. And the biggest *T. rex* in the world.

The Right Place for the Right Time

You can't find a *T. rex* just anywhere. Robert Gebhardt was lucky that he happened to hike over exactly the right spot in the badlands. We're all lucky that his eye was sharp enough to spot that little bit of tail bone that was sticking out of the ground. But finding Scotty wasn't only a matter of good luck and good eyesight. It was also good science. **Stratigraphy** is the science of how rock layers build up and crumble away over time. Today, there are places like the badlands where

In the badlands of Saskatchewan, you can see many prehistoric rock layers. Some of these rock layers are as old as dinosaurs, and many are filled with fossils.

This photo shows the hill where Robert Gebhardt made his discovery.

old rock layers are crumbling. There are also places, like many beaches and swamp bottoms, where new rock layers are forming. A dinosaur's bones could only be fossilized if it died in a place like that. So, if you want to find *Tyrannosaurus* bones, you need to look in *Tyrannosaurus*-age rocks. The rocks also need to have formed in the right kind of environment. You won't find *Tyrannosaurus* fossils buried in rocks that formed in the deep oceans. Or in rocks from a prehistoric desert. *Tyrannosaurus* did not live in the deep ocean or the desert. Mr. Gebhardt and the rest of the fossil hunters went to those Saskatchewan badlands because they knew the rock layers there formed 66 million years ago, the same time that *Tyrannosaurus* roamed the earth. They also knew those rock layers formed in *Tyrannosaurus* habitat.

A Toast to *T. rex*

Where did the name "Scotty" come from? Well, after the first few bones were discovered, a team of dinosaur diggers returned to the site. After a hard day of digging, the team realized that there was much more of the skeleton. Robert Gebhardt had found the tail. Now, the team had uncovered several teeth and part of the jaws. It seemed likely that most of the bones in between were also buried there. The team was thrilled and ready to celebrate. One of the diggers had been saving something special for just such an occasion. As the tired but excited fossil hunters gathered around the campfire, they passed around an old bottle of Scotch whisky. Everyone filled their cup, and the team toasted their success. Soon, the bottle of Scotch was empty. No one seems to remember who thought of it first, but by the end of the night, the *T. rex* had its name. "Scotty" honours that shared bottle of aged Scotch.

HE-REX OR SHE-REX

Is Scotty male or female? In many animals, males and females look pretty much the same. In other animals, there's a big difference in appearance. This is called **sexual dimorphism**. Sometimes, sexual dimorphism includes bones. For example, in many antelope species, only the males have skulls with large horns. In the sailfin lizard, only males have tail bones with tall spines. In us humans, and many other mammals, females have wider pelvic bones than males. A wider pelvis makes it a little easier to give birth. Unfortunately, *Tyrannosaurus* doesn't seem to have had any sexually dimorphic horns or spines. Because dinosaurs laid eggs, the hips of males and females were the same width.

Male lions are hairier than females. Only the males grow long manes.

Male antelope, like these impalas, grow long horns. The horns are used to shove and stab other males.

What about the size of Scotty? In many animals, one sex is often much larger than the other. In animals like lions, crocodiles, turkeys and gorillas, males are usually much bigger than females. Does the great size of Scotty mean it was probably male? Not necessarily. In other animals, like spotted hyenas, geckoes, eagles and tarantulas, the females are often larger. In still other animals, size has nothing to do with sex. For now, we can't tell if Scotty is a he or a she.

TEAM REX:
Tim Tokaryk
The Best Friend a *T. rex* Could Have

Finding Scotty turned out to be the easiest part. In the years that followed, digging up the bones and getting them ready for research would be hard and extremely slow work. The digging required power tools, teams of volunteers and bulldozers. To store and clean the fossils, the Royal Saskatchewan Museum had to develop a brand new field station, right in the little town of Eastend. That town would go on to raise over a million dollars to build the *T. rex* Discovery Centre, a new museum for Scotty to call home.

Tim Tokaryk was there to help with it all. He led the digging and the fossil identification. He also worked hard to make sure that folks in Saskatchewan, the Canadian government and people throughout the world knew about Scotty and understood how exciting its discovery was. That was important, because digging up a dinosaur as big as Scotty takes a lot of volunteers and a lot of money. During the dig, Tim even gave tours of the **quarry** (the dig site) to local school groups and to visiting tourists. From Eastend, Saskatchewan, to Tokyo, Japan, Tim made Scotty big news. Getting the *T. rex* out of the ground and put on public display was a dream that Tim Tokaryk made come true.

Fossil bone is fragile. To dig it up, the team had to go slowly and carefully. Diggers kept bottles of glue on hand, just in case something broke.

The 66 million-year-old teeth of Scotty poke out of the earth.

Hard Rock

Digging up the skeleton of a dinosaur as large as *T. rex* is never an easy job. But some digs are harder than others. Scotty's bones were buried in the ancient sand of a prehistoric river. Over millions of years, that river sand had dried out and turned into **sandstone** ... really hard sandstone! The rocks that surrounded

Scotty's bones were all buried at the same depth within the rock. To reach that depth, a big chunk of the hillside had to go.

Scotty were like solid concrete. Digging through that tough rock required paleontologists to chip away at it with steel chisels and even motorized jackhammers. All this digging took more than five years. Once the bones were dug up, they still needed to be cleaned. The sandstone that clung close to the bones was all carefully removed. Scotty was first found in 1991, but its bones were not in a fit state to be studied by scientists or displayed to the public until 2014. That was 23 years of chiselling!

Paleontologists Tim Tokaryk (left) and Dr. John Storer (right) examine a new fossil in the badlands.

After being given a protective covering of white plaster and dragged out of the quarry, the biggest bones had to be lifted by a crane. The crane loaded the bones onto a truck so they could be driven home to the museum.

Horse Power

Not only was the sandstone that surrounded Scotty's skeleton really hard, it was also really heavy. Paleontologists can never completely remove all the rock from around a fossil right there at the dig site. That requires very careful work with fine tools back in the laboratory. Instead, we usually chisel out large blocks of rock with the fossils still inside of them. We wrap these blocks in cloth that has been soaked in wet plaster. The plaster soon dries out and hardens to form a protective shell around the fossil block. We call this a **plaster jacket**. The plaster jacket keeps the block and, more importantly, the fossils inside it from breaking apart while it's transported to the lab.

The biggest plaster jackets in the Scotty quarry were too heavy for the field team to lift. So, they tried to bring in a tractor to pull them out. But there are no roads in the badlands, and the hillsides around the quarry were steep. The tractor couldn't get close enough to the quarry. The field team thought it over. They decided to try to do things the old-fashioned way. They brought in a team of horses. The horses could walk down the steep slopes of the badlands

A team of horses was given the tough job of hauling out the biggest fossil block.

and get right next to the fossil blocks. The diggers tied a rope around the biggest plaster jacket and then tied the other end to the team of horses. It was no easy pull, but the horses were strong enough to move what the paleontologists couldn't.

Treasures Mapped

While digging in a fossil quarry, paleontologists always make a map of where each bone is found. A quarry map can tell you some important things about the fossils you're digging up. Have a look at the map of the Scotty quarry. Can you see how the skeleton should be pieced back together?

Yeah, it's pretty hard to tell. The bones look like they're all jumbled up.

This quarry map shows where every bone was found. You can see the skeleton is all a big mess! The flow of a prehistoric river pushed the bones into two big piles.

The leg bones aren't all together. Part of the skull is right next to part of the hip. There are ribs and **vertebrae** all over the place! Clearly, when the skeleton got buried, it was **disarticulated.** "Disarticulated" means separated, with the bones no longer connected together as they would have been in life. That tells us Scotty probably didn't get buried in the sandbar right after it died. Instead, Scotty's body must have lain out above ground long enough for the muscles and **ligaments** that held its skeleton together to rot away. Then, the bones probably got swept away by a fast-flowing, flooding river. A peaceful, slow-flowing river would not have been strong enough to carry away the largest of the bones found at the quarry. Maybe this happened during a big rainstorm, when a river was overflowing with extra water. As the fast-flowing water carried along the bones, they got jumbled up. Finally, the water carrying the disarticulated skeleton arrived at the sandbar. The water slowed down. The bones stuck and then sank into the sand.

Missing Pieces

Paleontologists hardly ever find the complete skeletons of big dinosaurs. Scotty was no exception. Although paleontologists unearthed most of Scotty's skeleton, nearly 35 per cent of the bones were never found. These pieces aren't missing because paleontologists stopped digging too soon or overlooked them. Probably, these bones never fossilized, or they were destroyed long before Scotty was discovered. **Taphonomy** is the scientific study of what happens to the bodies of prehistoric animals after death. Make no mistake: much can happen.

A dead *Tyrannosaurus* would be an appetizing meal for many smaller meat eaters. Some of Scotty's skeleton might

Lying dead in a river channel, Scotty's body must have attracted scavengers. Soon, it would also start to rot.

have been eaten and carried away by **scavengers**. Maybe some of the bones were swept away by the river before they could be buried in the ancient sandbar. Even the bones that did get buried and fossilized were not safe. After 65 million years, when part of the fossil skeleton was exposed on the surface, it could erode. **Erosion** is when natural processes like freezing and thawing, falling rain and blowing wind wear away rocks and soil. If paleontologists don't find fossils right when the rocks around them start to erode, then the fossils themselves will also start eroding.

A Grave Error

Have a look at this little bone. It's part of a finger, and it was found mixed in among all the other bones at the Scotty quarry. Compared to its huge body, a *Tyrannosaurus* had tiny arms and teeny-tiny finger bones. Because the finger bones of a *Tyrannosaurus* are so small, they're much rarer fossils than other parts of the skeleton. Tiny bones could be easily picked up by scavengers or washed away by flowing water. After fossilization, small bones also erode quickly after they're exposed. So, when the digging team found this little finger bone, they got very excited. It seemed that they'd found a rare part of a *Tyrannosaurus* skeleton.

But no such luck! After careful examination, it was clear that this little finger bone didn't belong to a *Tyrannosaurus* at all. Instead, it belonged to the hand of a *Struthiomimus* (see pages 104–105). *Struthiomimus* was an herbivorous dinosaur that lived at the same time as Scotty. *Struthiomimus* was much smaller than *Tyrannosaurus*. It was about the size of a modern ostrich, but it had large arms and fingers compared to the size of its body. So, little *Struthiomimus* had arms and fingers that were about the same size as a big *Tyrannosaurus*'s. No other *Struthiomimus* bones were found at the Scotty quarry. It seems that this one finger bone had been washed in from somewhere else.

Actual Size

This is the only finger bone discovered at the Scotty quarry.

TEAM REX:
Wes Long
Shovelling and Scribing

Wes Long has probably spent more time working on Scotty's bones than anyone else. Wes is a fossil **excavator** and **preparator**. An excavator is someone who digs. Although a few of Scotty's bones were exposed on the ground, most were buried deep in the hillside. Every summer for years, Wes and other excavators hiked through the badlands to the Scotty quarry. There, they dug as best they could through the hard stone that the bones were buried in.

However, most of Wes's time with Scotty wasn't spent at the quarry. As a preparator, Wes spent the rest of the year cleaning Scotty's bones in the laboratory. Wes's preparation work started by cutting into a plaster jacket and revealing a block from the quarry. Then, he used an **air scribe** to carefully chip apart little bits of rock that surrounded the *Tyrannosaurus* bones. An air scribe looks like a thick metal pencil with a flexible tube running out the back end. That tube is attached to a machine that squeezes bursts of air through the tube. Those bursts vibrate the tip of the pencil. When squeezed hard and fast, the bursts of air turn the air scribe into a miniature jackhammer that is powerful enough to chip through even metal. That was just what Wes needed to break up the sturdy sandstone clinging to Scotty's bones.

This is an air scribe. It's used to break apart very hard rock.

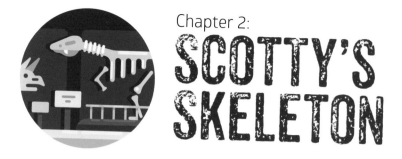

Chapter 2

SCOTTY'S SKELETON

Big, Bigger, Biggest

Once Scotty's bones had been dug up and carefully cleaned, scientists could finally start studying them. We could also start trying to put the skeleton back together. Paleontologists measured the bones and compared them to other fossil skeletons. Over fifty other skeletons of

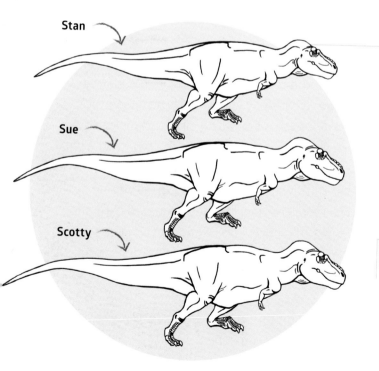

Stan

Sue

Scotty

Some *T. rex* are larger than others. These are three of the biggest.

The *T. rex* known as "Stan" has unusually long femora (upper leg bones). That makes it a very tall *T. rex*.

Tyrannosaurus have now been found. Just as we humans all look a little different, so did all *Tyrannosaurus*. Two of the biggest *Tyrannosaurus* skeletons are nicknamed "Stan" and "Sue" (but, as with Scotty, we don't know if they were male or female). Stan was an unusually tall *Tyrannosaurus*, with long and skinny legs. Sue was a little shorter, but overall much bigger. Sue had thick bones and would have outweighed Stan. Scotty was more similar to Sue. Scotty also had very thick bones and would have been heavier than Stan. In fact, Scotty was a bit heavier than Sue and also just a little taller and longer. Paleontologists estimate that Scotty weighed over 8,600 kilograms. That's more than 50 African lions or 20 polar bears! So far, Scotty is the biggest *Tyrannosaurus* ever found.

MESOZOIC ERA
THE AGE OF DINOSAURS

Queen's Ransom

Like Scotty, the *T. rex* named "Sue" has thick bones. Sue was a heavyweight and is the most complete *T. rex* skeleton ever found. Sue's skeleton can be seen at the Field Museum in Chicago.

The *Tyrannosaurus* nicknamed "Sue" is nearly as big as Scotty and is even more complete—nearly 90 per cent. Sue is on display at the Field Museum in Chicago. To get Sue, the Field Museum had to pay a high price. Sue was discovered in the state of South Dakota. As in most of the United States, fossils in South Dakota belong to whoever owns the land they're buried in. Rather than donate Sue, the landowner decided to sell the skeleton. How much did Sue cost? Over eight million dollars! Did Scotty have a similar cost? No. Scotty was found in Canada. In Canada, all dinosaur skeletons legally belong to everyone. This means that skeletons can't be sold and must go to a museum or university that will study them and put them on public display. The Royal Saskatchewan Museum had to put a lot of hard work into digging Scotty up, but there was no extra fee.

How to Copy a Fossil

When putting entire dinosaur skeletons on display, museums often don't use the actual fossils. Real dinosaur fossils are extremely heavy (remember, they're filled with rock) and are much easier for paleontologists to study if they haven't been put back together into a towering skeleton. Instead, museums make **casts**—extremely accurate copies of fossils made out of lightweight material, like plastic. To make a cast, you start with the real fossil and pour a thick liquid (which looks a little like pudding) all over it. The liquid completely covers the fossil on all sides

Scotty's bones get a good gooping. That goop will dry into a mould.

The last step in creating a fossil cast is to give the dry cast a coat of paint.

and hardens into a thick, rubbery mould. Then you carefully cut open the mould and remove the fossil. With the fossil gone, the rubbery mould now has a hole that's the exact shape of the fossil.

Then, you pour a liquid polymer (which usually looks like milk or warm honey) into that fossil-shaped hole. After the polymer hardens, you remove it from the mould, and presto! You've made a lightweight fossil cast. Another great thing about fossil casts is that you can make as many as you want. That means the Royal Saskatchewan Museum can send copies of Scotty's bones to other museums, where many other scientists can examine and study them.

Filling in the Gaps

The Royal Saskatchewan Museum wanted to put Scotty's skeleton on display. They could make casts of all the bones that had been found, but what about the 35 per cent of the bones that were missing? Well, think about your own body for a moment. Your right side is very similar to your left side—just flipped around. That includes your skeleton. Your right arm has all the same bones as your left, and they're usually not very different. Knowing what Scotty's right **femur** (the upper leg bone) looked like, the Royal Saskatchewan Museum knew basically what Scotty's left femur would have looked like. So, they could make a copy of the left based on the right. For the missing bones without a left or a right match, the Royal Saskatchewan Museum had to replicate them based on other *Tyrannosaurus* skeletons, but enlarged to fit Scotty's size.

About 65 per cent of Scotty's bones were found (shown in brown). But thanks to other *T. rex* skeletons, we know what the missing pieces look like.

TEAM REX:
Jon Runolfson
Model Maker

Putting together the skeleton of an enormous *Tyrannosaurus* is a big job. Before you start, you need to make a plan. You need to be sure the skeleton will fit into the room where you're going to display it. The Royal Saskatchewan Museum also wanted to make sure that once Scotty's skeleton was assembled, it would be standing in a pose that was scientifically accurate. So, they turned to Jon Runolfson. Jon created tiny copies of the bones in Scotty's skeleton. He then assembled the complete skeleton by sticking the little bones on a wire frame. That frame could be bent and adjusted. Next, he built a tiny model of the room that the skeleton needed to fit in. Now, Jon could place his little *Tyrannosaurus* inside the little museum and bend the dinosaur into different positions. As he experimented, he checked with me to make sure that he was putting the *Tyrannosaurus* in a natural pose. Once Jon had every miniature detail just right, the Royal Saskatchewan Museum assembled the big skeleton to match.

This little *T. rex* model helped us to get Scotty's pose just right.

Standing Tall

When deciding how to display their dinosaurs, museums have more to worry about than just making sure a skeleton is put together realistically. Most predators spend a great deal of their time sleeping. It would have been realistic for the Royal Saskatchewan Museum to pose Scotty lying down and taking a nap. But museums also want their dinosaurs to be exciting for visitors to look at. *Tyrannosaurus rex* did lots of exciting things and there are many cool ways its skeleton can be posed that are also realistic. To impress visitors, museums like their *T. rex* skeletons to be standing up, heads towering high in the

This photo shows the fully assembled skeleton of Scotty, as seen from the balcony at the Royal Saskatchewan Museum.

air. However, the part of *T. rex* that most visitors want a good look at is the skull and the rows of huge teeth. That means the head needs to be where visitors can get close to it.

To get the head down to human eye level, I saw one museum pose their *T. rex* bending over to feed on a dead *Triceratops*. Others have posed *T. rex* roaring at the ground, squatting and even sitting down. When I helped the Royal Saskatchewan Museum decide how to pose Scotty, we came up with a different idea. The museum raised the ceiling in Scotty's exhibit and built a balcony. The skeleton is posed standing at its full height. You should go see it. You can walk into the exhibit and get a sense of what it would be like to stand beside such a massive dinosaur. And then, you can climb some stairs up to the balcony for a face-to-face look.

From the balcony in the Royal Saskatchewan Museum exhibit, you can have a close encounter with Scotty's skull and teeth.

TEAM REX:
Beth Zaiken
Royal Portrait

Just like everyone else, paleontologists want to picture what dinosaurs looked like when they were alive. To do that, we scientists usually need help from a talented artist. A **paleoartist** is an illustrator who specializes in prehistoric life. Beth Zaiken (who painted the pictures of Scotty in this book) is one of the best.

Being a good paleoartist means trying to make your illustrations as scientifically accurate as possible. That takes more than just a paintbrush and artistic talent. If you draw *Tyrannosaurus*, you need to make sure its legs are the right size compared to its body, that its tail is the right length, that its jaw muscles bulge in just the right way, and many more tiny details. So, you need to learn a great deal about paleontology (and it helps to know a lot about the appearance

Beth paints the sky over a herd of prehistoric wild horses at the Ancient Ozarks Natural History Museum.

We don't know what colour Scotty was, but that's no excuse to just paint it whatever colour you want. By looking at modern animals, you can make a smart guess.

of modern animals). Paleoartists work with paleontologists who are experts on the specific prehistoric animal they're trying to illustrate. Bit by bit, the scientist and the artist work together to adjust the details of a prehistoric illustration. The result is the best picture that we can come up with of how that dinosaur, mammoth, ancient fern or other prehistoric species would have looked in life.

Naturally, there's much about how Scotty looked that Beth and I don't know. For instance, Beth has coloured Scotty a pale green, and she's given Scotty some faint stripes. I think that's a good guess. Being a predator, Scotty would need to be **camouflaged**. Scotty lived in a land lush with plants, so green was probably the best colour for hiding. Many predators also have stripes to help them blend in with their surroundings. Then again, many camouflaged predators have splotches or spots instead. We don't yet know what colour a *Tyrannosaurus* really was. For now, all paleontologists and paleoartists can do is make our best guess.

Scotty's Crown

If I asked you to name a horned dinosaur, you'd probably say "*Triceratops*" or maybe "*Torosaurus*," but "*Tyrannosaurus*" is also a correct answer. *Tyrannosaurus* didn't have great big horns, but it did have several little spikes and bony lumps on its face. You can see these horns on Scotty's skull. Scotty's biggest horn is called the **postorbital boss**. This is a thick knob of bone, just behind and above Scotty's eyes. Scotty also had a pair of **jugal horns**. A jugal horn is a spike that sticks out from each of Scotty's cheek bones. Like the horns of a bull, goat or antelope, Scotty's horns were made of bone and also had an outer covering of the material that your fingernails are made of. This material

Postorbital Boss

Jugal Horn

Scotty's face had many small horns.

is called **keratin**, and it can be very sharp. What were the postorbital boss and jugal horns for? Scotty probably did not try to head-butt its prey (the jaws of a *Tyrannosaurus* would be much better weapons). Probably, the horns helped protect Scotty. The postorbital boss was a natural helmet, in case Scotty ever got kicked, bitten or tail-slapped on the top of its head. The spiky jugal horns may have made other *Tyrannosaurus* think twice before biting Scotty's face.

Belly Ribs

Most of the bones in a *Tyrannosaurus* skeleton are the same bones that are in your skeleton, just much bigger and often differently shaped. Like you, a *Tyrannosaurus* had ribs, vertebrae, phalanges (the little bones in fingers and toes) and so on. But *Tyrannosaurus* also had a few bones that you don't have. **Gastralia** are one example. Gastralia are also called "belly ribs," and they grew in the skin of the belly. *Tyrannosaurus* had a long stack of gastralia that ran from its hips to its lower chest. What were they for? The gastralia probably formed a hard wall that protected the belly and helped to support the dinosaur's big guts. However, *Tyrannosaurus* also had muscles attached to its gastralia. These muscles could move the gastralia. Many paleontologists think that by flexing and relaxing its belly ribs, *Tyrannosaurus* could take bigger breaths. So, having gastralia helped Scotty breathe.

See those little bones all along Scotty's belly? Those are gastralia.

TEAM REX:
Dr. Gregory Erickson
Long Lived

There's a great deal to be learned from Scotty's skeleton, but sometimes you have to look *very* closely. Dr. Gregory Erickson is a world-famous expert in dinosaur **bone histology**, the study of bone through a microscope. The Royal Saskatchewan Museum called in Dr. Erickson and asked him to take a tiny sample of bone from Scotty's leg. Dr. Erickson ground that sample of bone down until it was so thin that light could shine through it. Finally, he stuck it under a microscope and had a look.

The leg bones of all animals have a large hollow space in their centre, where blood and nerves run. Carnivorous dinosaur leg bones have extra-large hollow spaces, just like birds'. In life, these extra big hollow spaces helped make the bones lighter. As dinosaurs grew, their leg bones got larger and so did the hollow spaces. If you could watch a dinosaur bone grow in fast-forward under an X-ray machine, it would look like an inflating balloon. The bone's outer surface would expand and so would the inner hole, all at the same time. Bones can grow like this because they add new material to the outside and absorb old material from around the inner hole.

Growing bone requires energy and nutrients. So, a growing dinosaur needed plenty of food. In nature, food is often more available during some parts of the year (like summer and spring) than at other

Bone is complex stuff. At the centre of every big bone is a lot of blood and fat (the pink part). Spongy bone, with many holes, is not very strong but it's lightweight. Bone gets bigger by growing thin outer layers. These thin layers can build up, like the stacked pages of a book.

times (like winter, or during a drought). That means Dr. Erickson usually sees many different layers throughout the same bone sample. Usually, there are thick layers of bone that grew quickly during times when there was lots of food, and thin layers of bone that grew slowly during times when food was less available.

But all of Scotty's bone looked the same. There were no layers. This was unusual, but Dr. Erickson knew what it meant—Scotty was old when it died. Scotty's hadn't been adding new material to the outside of its bones because Scotty didn't need to grow anymore. It was a full-sized adult. Even layers left over from Scotty's youth were gone because they'd become worn out and had been slowly replaced. That meant Scotty had been fully grown for several years. All this told Dr. Erickson that Scotty was the longest-lived *Tyrannosaurus* ever found. Dr. Erickson then compared Scotty's bone growth pattern to that of other *Tyrannosaurus*. He discovered that Scotty was probably a little over thirty years old when it finally died.

Old Wounds

Imagine if you were a *Tyrannosaurus*. What a rough and challenging life that would be! Growing up, all sorts of toothy things, like big crocodiles, raptor dinosaurs and other *Tyrannosaurus* would want to eat you. Most herbivorous dinosaurs would be looking to stomp you out before you could get big enough to eat them. Even as an adult, you would have to get food by attacking other huge and powerful dinosaurs—many with armoured weapons. It's no surprise that Scotty's skeleton has many **pathologies**. A pathology is damage to a body from injury or sickness. In this case, it is an oddly shaped bit of bone that shows where the skeleton was

Actual Size

Rib Break

This is one of Scotty's ribs. See that lumpy part? That's not normal. This is a spot where the rib was broken and didn't heal perfectly.

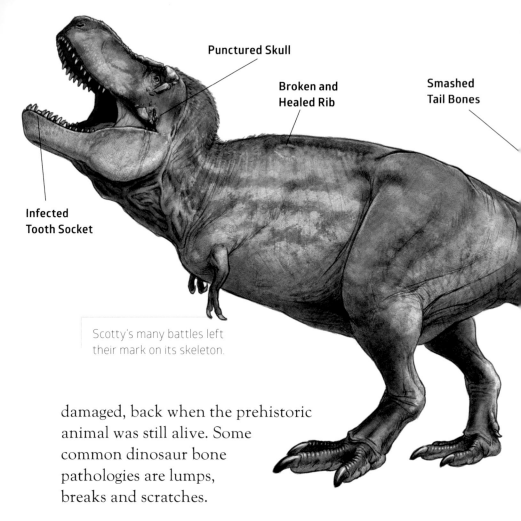

Punctured Skull

Broken and
Healed Rib

Smashed
Tail Bones

Infected
Tooth Socket

Scotty's many battles left
their mark on its skeleton.

damaged, back when the prehistoric
animal was still alive. Some
common dinosaur bone
pathologies are lumps,
breaks and scratches.

Eaten from
the Inside Out

Scotty had much to worry about: the horns of *Triceratops*,
the armoured tail clubs of *Ankylosaurus* and even the teeth
of another *Tyrannosaurus*. But sometimes, it's the little things
that get you. Just like all animals, the "king of the dinosaurs"
was in danger from many kinds of viruses, bacteria or other
tiny **parasites**. Parasites are harmful living things that attach
themselves to other living things. One of Scotty's strangest

pathologies is a round hole in its right lower jaw. This hole goes all the way through the jaw bone, and there's no evidence of healing. Today, veterinarians sometimes see birds with similar jaw holes. The holes are created by a microscopic parasite called *Trichomonas*. This nasty parasite eats away at a bird's mouth and may even spread to its organs. Scotty is not the only *Tyrannosaurus* to have suffered from this parasite. Several other *Tyrannosaurus*, including Sue, have many more and larger diseased jaw holes.

These round holes on Scotty's jaw bones are bad news. They mark infection by a bone-eating parasite.

The skull is not just one bone. It's made of many bones that fit tightly together, like the pieces of a jigsaw puzzle. Often, fossil skulls are found still pieced together. But not Scotty's.

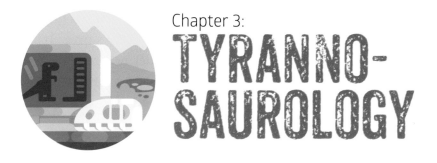

Chapter 3:
TYRANNO-SAUROLOGY

Evolution in Action

A *T. rex* like Scotty was a predator that had been fine-tuned over 160 million years of dinosaur **evolution**. Evolution is the natural process that changes species over time. Eventually, a species may change so much that it becomes a new species. Let's look at how this process works.

Like all living things, dinosaurs were good at making more of themselves. One mother duck-billed dinosaur could lay more than thirty eggs in one nest! However, only very few of those baby dinosaurs survived long enough to produce young of their own. Which ones made

You and Scotty both evolved from a little animal like this *Protorothyris*. It lived 298 million years ago.

48

The ancestors of all dinosaurs were small crawling reptiles. Over millions of years, some evolved to stand and run on just their two back legs. Eventually, some also grew bigger and bigger. Their jaws got stronger and stronger and their arms shrank.

it? Well, all the baby dinosaurs of a particular species were not exactly the same. They were each a little different. Some of these differences were advantages. Maybe one dinosaur had a beak that was a little bit harder, making the dinosaur a little better at munching ferns. Or maybe another dinosaur had legs that were slightly longer, making it a little bit faster. The specific dinosaurs that had these advantages were more likely to be the ones that survived and got to lay eggs.

Now, here is the key fact that makes evolution work. Many of the children of those dinosaurs that had harder beaks and longer legs would *also* have hard beaks and long legs. This is called **inheritance**. What you look, sound and act like has a lot to do with who your parents are. You're not identical to your parents, but you have many similarities. Has anyone ever told you that you have your father's nose, or your mother's smile? If so, those are probably **traits** you've inherited from your parents. Just like their parents, the young hard-beaked and long-legged dinosaurs had an advantage. Dinosaurs with softer beaks and shorter legs were more likely to die early before producing young. Eventually, only hard-beaked, long-legged dinosaurs would be left. They would continue to produce hard-beaked, long-legged babies. That process could repeat. Maybe some of the hard-beaked, long-legged dinosaurs had beaks that were a bit harder still, or legs that were just a little bit longer. Or maybe, there was some other new trait with a new advantage, like sharper horns. Eventually, super-hard-beaked, super-long-legged and super-sharp-horned dinosaurs evolved. These dinosaurs were so different from the earlier soft-beaked, short-legged, dull-horned dinosaurs that they had become … a new species!

Tyrannosaurus

Daspletosaurus

Gorgosaurus

Tyrannosaurids

Birds

Dilong

Deinonychosaurs

Tyrannosauroids

Ornithomimids

Coelurosaurs

Allosaurids

Spinosaurs

Ceratosaurs

Theropods

Sauropodomorphs

Dinosaurs

Over enough time, species may evolve to be so different from their ancestors that it becomes hard to tell they're related. You and a *T. rex* don't look alike, but you are related. Your shared ancestor lived over 300 million years ago and was a little scaly creature that laid eggs and liked to eat insects.

Family Relations

This diagram shows where *Tyrannosaurus* fits on the dinosaur family tree. Scientists group dinosaurs (and all other living things) based on their **evolutionary relationships**. Species that haven't changed much since they split away from their shared ancestors (and so still look very similar) are placed together in a small group. Many small groups may be combined to form larger groups that include dinosaurs that are more distantly related. For example, have a look at this tree, and you will see that *Tyrannosaurus* and its close relatives, like *Daspletosaurus* and *Gorgosaurus*, belong together in a small group called the **tyrannosaurids**. Together with more distant relatives, like *Dilong*, the tyrannosaurids belong to a larger group called the **tyrannosauroids** (note the O, making the word rhyme with "asteroids"). Tyrannosauroids, birds, deinonychosaurs and ornithomimids are all members

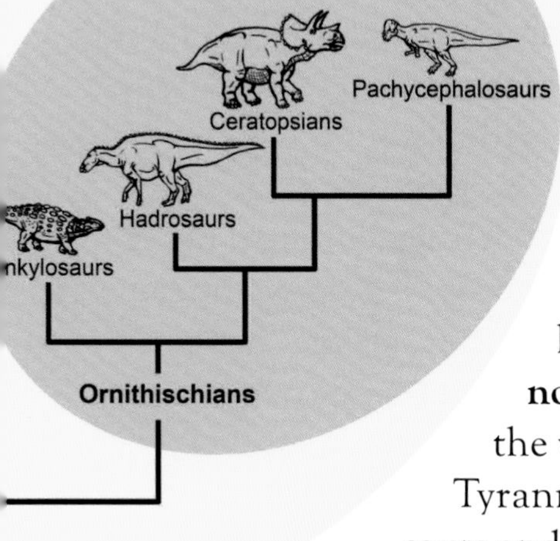

Pachycephalosaurs

Ceratopsians

Hadrosaurs

nkylosaurs

Ornithischians

of a group called the coelurosaurs. And all carnivorous dinosaurs belong to a very large group called the theropods.

Scotty is a *Tyrannosaurus*. That means Scotty is also a tyrannosaurid, a tyrannosauroid, a coelurosaur, a theropod and a dinosaur. However, Scotty is not a bird, a sauropodomorph or an ornithischian.

What's in a Name?

Two of the very smallest groups that an animal can belong to are called **genus** and **species**. Animals that belong in the same genus are so closely related that their skeletons are nearly identical. They also usually eat the same kinds of food and have very similar behaviours. For example, lions and tigers have skeletons that are extremely difficult to tell apart, and they're both big cats and predators. Lions and tigers belong to the same genus, *Panthera*. But lions and tigers aren't exactly the same. They're separate species within the *Panthera* genus. Animals that belong to the same species are even more similar to each other, so similar that the males and females can have healthy babies. Within one genus, there may be many different species.

Scientists give every species (be it a dinosaur, kangaroo, jellyfish, plant, mushroom or bacterium) a special two-part name. These scientific names are called **binomials**. They combine the name of the creature's genus with a second name called the **specific epithet**. For example, the scientific name of the African lion is *Panthera leo*. Your scientific binomial name is *Homo sapiens*, and so is mine, since we belong to the same species. The first part of our name, *Homo*, means "human." The second part, *sapiens*, means "wise." *Homo* is our genus name and *sapiens* is our specific epithet.

We're very closely related to many extinct species that looked similar to us. For example, our prehistoric relatives

Homo erectus and *Homo habilis* are so like us that they belong to the same genus (and have the same genus name). It's a rule that once a name has been given to one genus, that same name can't be given to another genus. It's also a rule that no two species within the same genus can have the same specific epithet. However, sometimes, species that belong to different genera do have the same specific epithet—like the sabre-toothed cat *Smilodon gracilis* and the duck *Anas gracilis*. Why are their specific epithets the same? Well, *gracilis* means "slender." *Anas gracilis* is a bit skinnier than the ducks it's most closely related to, and *Smilodon gracilis* has skinny teeth compared with other sabre-toothed cats. What matters is that the complete binomial is unique.

This is our close relative *Homo habilis*. We didn't just look alike—we also thought alike. *Homo habilis* had a big brain and made tools. It carved stones into knives and used them to skin its food.

Because binomials are long, scientists often abbreviate them. For example, *Homo sapiens* can be abbreviated to *H. sapiens*. In the binomial *Tyrannosaurus rex*, *Tyrannosaurus* is the genus name and *rex* is the specific epithet. *Tyrannosaurus rex* can be abbreviated to *T. rex*. For now, only one species of *Tyrannosaurus* is known. So, the names *Tyrannosaurus* and *Tyrannosaurus rex* (or *T. rex*) mean the same thing.

Dr. Henry Fairfield Osborn

Titling a Tyrant

Dr. Henry Fairfield Osborn was one of the world's greatest dinosaur paleontologists. He worked at the American Museum of Natural History in New York City. There, he designed dinosaur exhibits that millions of people came to see. Osborn named many new species of dinosaurs and other prehistoric animals. The most famous of all his names is *Tyrannosaurus rex*. Just how do you get to name a new dinosaur? Well, it's not easy. You have to do more than just find it. In fact, it doesn't even matter if you find it. Dr. Osborn didn't find *Tyrannosaurus rex*. Instead, the first *T. rex* skeleton was found by Barnum Brown, who worked for Dr. Osborn. To name a new dinosaur, you have to explain to other paleontologists why the dinosaur is new and different. That means you have to write a description of the dinosaur's skeleton. The description must point out the differences between the new skeleton and the skeletons of other, already-named dinosaurs. You can use illustrations and photographs as part of your description.

You can't just keep this description in your desk drawer, either. You have to get it into a **scientific publication**. A scientific publication is a collection of reports that shares research results. But getting your writing into a scientific publication isn't easy. To make sure no one's publishing wrong information, scientific publications usually ask other scientists to review your work. If these other scientists decide that your description is incomplete or unconvincing, then it won't be published.

In 1905, Dr. Osborn published his scientific description of *T. rex*. In that description, Dr. Osborn gave the new dinosaur its name. He was so impressed with how large and terrifying the animal was that he chose the name *Tyrannosaurus rex*. In ancient Greek, *Tyrannosaurus* means "tyrant lizard." In Latin, the language of ancient Rome, *rex* means "king."

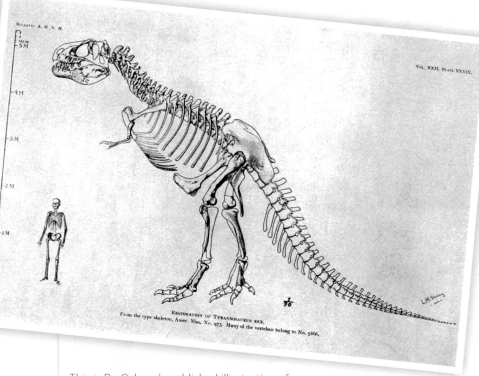

This is Dr. Osborn's published illustration of the first *T. rex* skeleton.

Humble Beginnings

One hundred and sixty-six million years ago (one hundred million years before *Tyrannosaurus rex*), the tyrannosauroids were not big dinosaurs. Most were smaller than a modern lion, and many were smaller than a wolf. Other kinds of carnivorous dinosaurs lived at the same time. These other carnivores included huge species, some larger than rhinos or elephants.

Early tyrannosauroids had to hunt small animals while avoiding those bigger predators. They were good at it. They might not have been big, but even early tyrannosauroids shared some traits with *T. rex*:

1. Long leg bones
2. Big hip bones
3. Stiff tail tips

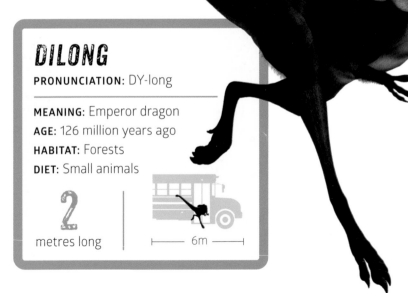

DILONG

PRONUNCIATION: DY-long

MEANING: Emperor dragon
AGE: 126 million years ago
HABITAT: Forests
DIET: Small animals

2 metres long

6m

A STEP AHEAD

When you walk or run, your legs swing out in front, your feet touch the ground and your leg muscles pull you forward. Today, animals that are fast runners tend to have long legs compared to their body size. Long legs make every swing and step cover more ground. When you look at dinosaurs, pay attention to the length of their leg bones. Like modern animals, faster dinosaurs had longer legs. Tyrannosauroids had some of the longest leg bones of any kind of dinosaur. With their long legs, they could chase and catch almost any prey they wanted.

HIP TO MOVE

Compared to many other carnivorous dinosaurs, tyrannosauroids have big hip bones. The hip bones (or the **pelvis**) are important bones when it comes to moving around. The femur (the upper leg bone) attaches to the pelvis. This

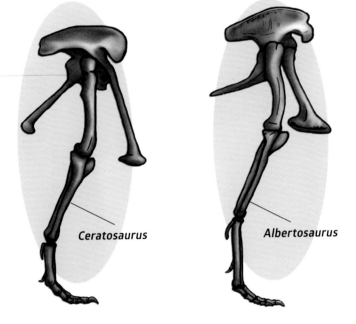

The leg and hip bones of the big carnivorous dinosaur *Ceratosaurus* (not a tyrannosauroid) and *Albertosaurus* (a tyrannosauroid).

Ceratosaurus

Albertosaurus

attachment controls how the leg swings when walking and running. Just as importantly, many upper leg muscles also attach to the pelvis. By having big hip bones, tyrannosauroids had room for big leg muscles. Bigger leg muscles mean stronger legs. The large pelvis of tyrannosauroids is an important clue that tells us tyrannosauroids were faster runners than most other predatory dinosaurs.

EPIC TAIL

What good is a tail? For some dinosaurs, the tail was a weapon that had spikes or armour on its tip. Some dinosaurs had fans of tail feathers and waved their tails in mating dances. For most dinosaurs, the tail was important because it provided the power to walk and run. Like modern lizards and crocodiles, dinosaurs had huge muscles at the base of their tail. These muscles attached to their leg bones. Just like the big leg muscles that attached to the pelvis, the leg muscles that attached to the tail were key to a dinosaur's movement.

This is one bone from the tail of the tyrannosauroid *Gorgosaurus*. A tyrannosauroid tail is made up of many bones like this and the long prongs helped hold the bones together.

Tyrannosauroids had large leg muscles in the front half of their tail, but not in the back half. That's typical for most dinosaurs. What's not typical is the way the bones in the back half of a tyrannosauroid's tail connected to each other. Usually, the back half of a dinosaur's tail was flexible and could easily wiggle and shake in all directions. In the back half of a tyrannosauroid's tail, the tail bones fit together tightly. That made the tail stiff. Stiff tails were not wiggly, but they could easily be swung all at once. A tail like that would be useful for balance. If a tyrannosauroid started to fall or suddenly needed to shift its weight in a tight turn, a swift swing of the stiff tail could act as a helpful counterbalance.

Like all tyrannosauroids, *Dilong* had a tail that was flexible at the front but stiff towards the tip.

Rise of the Tyrannosaurids

Over time, some tyrannosauroids got bigger. This meant they were eating larger dinosaurs and were in competition with other large carnivores. As time went on, big tyrannosauroids survived and increased in number, while the other kinds of big carnivorous dinosaurs didn't. Besides getting bigger, tyrannosauroids changed in other ways. Eventually, the tyrannosaurid group evolved. Most tyrannosaurids looked much like *T. rex*. They all shared these traits:

1. Tiny hands and short arms
2. Extra-large jaws
3. Thick teeth

Teratophoneu.

Albertosaurus

Alioramus

Gorgosaurus

Qianzhousaurus

Tyrannosaurids

Appalachiosaurus

Dryptosaurus

Eotyrannus

Dilong

Proceratosaurus

Guanlong

Tyrannosauroids

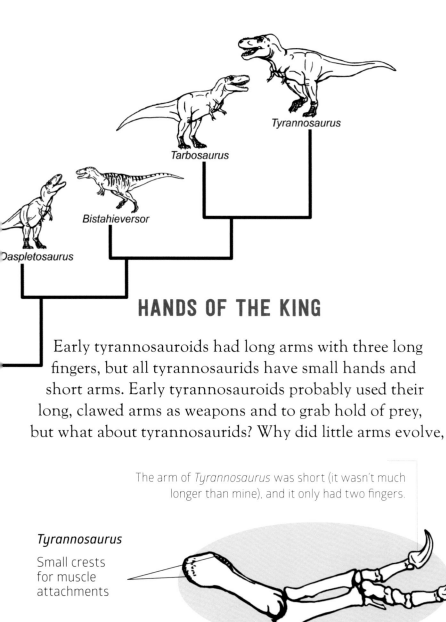

Tyrannosaurus

Tarbosaurus

Bistahieversor

Daspletosaurus

HANDS OF THE KING

Early tyrannosauroids had long arms with three long
fingers, but all tyrannosaurids have small hands and
short arms. Early tyrannosauroids probably used their
long, clawed arms as weapons and to grab hold of prey,
but what about tyrannosaurids? Why did little arms evolve,

The arm of *Tyrannosaurus* was short (it wasn't much
longer than mine), and it only had two fingers.

Tyrannosaurus

Small crests
for muscle
attachments

Allosaurus

Big crests
for muscle
attachments

and what good were they? The reach of a tyrannosaurid's arms was so short that, in order to grab on to another dinosaur, that other dinosaur would have to be nearly in the tyrannosaurid's lap. Even then, a struggling duckbill or *Triceratops* would have been far too strong to be held by such little arms.

Evolution doesn't always add new traits. It doesn't just keep making animals more and more complicated. If a trait, like long arms and fingers, is no longer useful, it's better to get rid of it. That way, you're not wasting energy in growing the trait. Probably, the arms, hands and finger claws of tyrannosaurids were not good for much of anything. In their role as weapons and grabbers, they had been replaced by powerful jaws and a very strong neck.

CRUNCH TIME

Of all the carnivorous dinosaurs, none had more dangerous bites than tyrannosaurids. Tyrannosaurids had wide openings at the backs of their skulls and on the sides of their jaws that provided huge spaces for enormous jaw muscles. These muscles gave tyrannosaurids exceptionally powerful bites.

But there was more to a tyrannosaurid bite than just its power. Tyrannosaurids also had special teeth. Most other carnivorous dinosaur teeth had a flat edge, like the blade of a knife. Tyrannosaurid teeth were much thicker. These thick

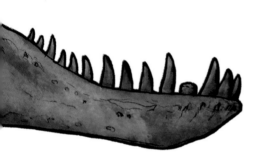

This is one of Scotty's teeth. It's thick with a round tip.

Actual Size

teeth were not as good at slicing off soft meat as the teeth of other carnivorous dinosaurs. However, tyrannosaurid teeth were extremely good at stabbing into bone. Biting right into hard bone would have broken most other dinosaurs' teeth. But the thick teeth of tyrannosaurids could handle it. Combined with the extra jaw power, tyrannosaurid teeth could sink deep into a dinosaur and crunch right through its skeleton!

In this *Gorgosaurus* jaw, you can see the tip of a new tooth growing underneath an old one.

TEETH TO SPARE

When fighting with other dinosaurs, did Scotty ever break a tooth? Yes. Even with extra-thick teeth, Scotty probably broke teeth often. But for a *Tyrannosaurus*, a broken tooth was no big deal. Like most dinosaurs, *Tyrannosaurus* was always growing new teeth. These new teeth grew right below the old ones. Eventually, a new tooth grew bigger and bigger until it popped out the old tooth and took its place. Then, another new tooth would start growing in below that one. This means that a broken tooth would not stick around very long. Even teeth that were just a little dull would be replaced by new, sharper ones.

Walking Softly

In movies and cartoons, *Tyrannosaurus rex* often stomps loudly about. Did Scotty really shake the ground with every step it took? No. Tyrannosaurid footprints prove that the feet of these big carnivores had large fleshy pads. These pads cushioned Scotty's steps. The pads probably helped it run over solid ground without hurting its feet and would also have made Scotty's footfalls quiet. Other dinosaurs probably saw Scotty before they heard it coming.

With three long forward-pointing toes, Scotty left tracks that look a lot like a giant chicken's.

Dr. Ariana Paulina
Brain Power

Dr. Paulina studies the minds of dinosaurs. That's not easy, because brains are soft and squishy organs that rot and don't normally fossilize. Luckily for her, the brain is also an organ that is tightly surrounded by bone. The hole in the skull where the brain sits is called the **cranial cavity**. If we could see the cranial cavity of a dinosaur's skull, we would have a good idea of how large its brain was and what the brain's shape was like. The question is, how can you see the cavity when it's tightly surrounded by bones?

One way would be to cut the skull in two and pop it apart, like two halves of a plastic Easter egg. But that would mean breaking a dinosaur skull.

Dr. Paulina has found a better way. She puts dinosaur skulls inside an X-ray machine. This lets her look at the cranial cavity without damaging the fossils.

Using this technique, Dr. Paulina has learned much about the brains of big carnivorous dinosaurs. Compared with all the other

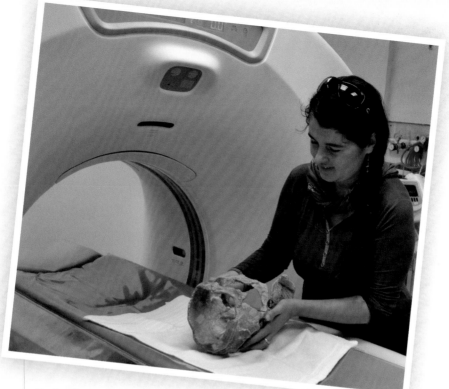

Dr. Paulina prepares
to send a fossil into the X-ray machine.

big meat-eating dinosaurs that she has X-rayed, *Tyrannosaurus* had
the biggest brain (even considering its large body size). That means
Tyrannosaurus was probably a smart dinosaur. It is likely that only a
few kinds of dinosaurs, like raptors and *Struthiomimus,* were smarter.
This also means *Tyrannosaurus* was much smarter than modern
reptiles like crocodiles, lizards and turtles. But don't get too excited.
Tyrannosaurus wasn't nearly as smart as a dog, a rhinoceros, a kangaroo or any modern bird. If you had Scotty as a pet, I bet you could
train it to come when you called and to do a few simple tricks like
"sit" and "stay." Could you train Scotty to do complicated jobs, like you
can train a collie to herd sheep or a German shepherd to search for
and rescue lost people? I doubt it. Scotty would probably just eat the
sheep. . . and the people.

The Better to See and Smell You With

By studying the shapes of dinosaur cranial cavities, paleontologists can tell what parts of a dinosaur's brain were especially large. One of the very largest parts of *T. rex*'s brain was the **olfactory bulb**. This is the part of the brain that makes sense of smells. Like a shark or a bloodhound, this dinosaur had a great sniffer. Scotty probably used smell to track down prey. The part of the brain that makes sense of information coming from the eyes was also really big. So *T. rex* had excellent eyesight.

The brain of Scotty.

Actual Size

Cerebellum: important for coordination and movement

Inner ear: important for hearing and balance

Brain stem: important for sending signals back and forth between the brain and body

Dino Sight

Try this experiment. Sit down at a table and place a pencil on the table in front of you. Now, close one eye and try to quickly touch the pencil's eraser with your finger. Sounds easy, but is it? You may be surprised to find that with only one eye open, this simple task becomes a little tricky. Why? Your left eye and your right eye have a slightly different view of the world. They see the same things but from slightly different angles. When both eyes look at an object, your brain uses the two slightly different views to help sense how far away that object is. We call this **depth perception**.

Did Scotty have good depth perception? Absolutely. The eyes of a *Tyrannosaurus rex* faced forward and almost everything it saw with the right eye was also seen by the left. Being able to keenly judge distances must have helped when lunging for prey or dodging the horns and tail clubs of other dinosaurs. But many dinosaurs did

Optic lobe: important for seeing

Cerebral hemisphere: important for complex behaviour and problem solving

Olfactory bulb: important for smelling

Pituitary: creates chemicals that are important for controlling growth, blood pressure and body temperature

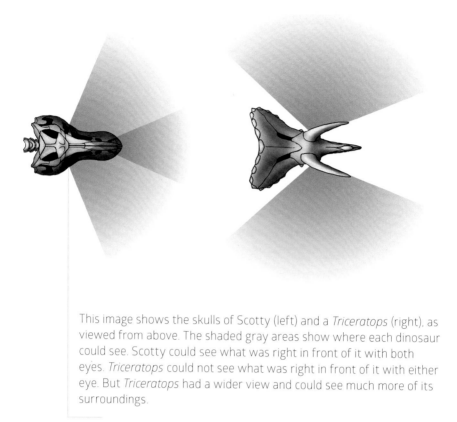

This image shows the skulls of Scotty (left) and a *Triceratops* (right), as viewed from above. The shaded gray areas show where each dinosaur could see. Scotty could see what was right in front of it with both eyes. *Triceratops* could not see what was right in front of it with either eye. But *Triceratops* had a wider view and could see much more of its surroundings.

not have keen depth perception. *Triceratops*, for example, had two big eyes that were spaced far apart, on either side of its head. Since the eyes were so far apart, what the right eye saw was very different from what the left eye saw. This means the brain of *Triceratops* could not combine its left and right eye vision to help perceive depth. That was bad, but, with both eyes facing different directions, *Triceratops* did have a much wider view. That was good. Plant-eating animals often have such sideways-positioned eyes. Wider views make it much easier to see danger approaching and much harder for a *T. rex* to sneak up on you.

Dr. Karen Chin
Who Dung It?

Dr. Karen Chin is an expert on dinosaur dung. She studies **coprolites**—fossilized poop! In Saskatchewan, she has studied one particularly big piece of dinosaur dung. It measures almost half a metre in length. That's much longer than a toilet bowl is wide! This sizable prehistoric poop comes from a rock layer dating back 66 million years. It was less than two kilometres from the Scotty quarry. Looking at the coprolite under a microscope, Dr. Chin could see that it was chock full of tiny bits of dinosaur bone. So, it must have come from a large carnivore that had jaws powerful enough to pulverize bones before swallowing them. Based on all this evidence, it seems the coprolite was left behind by none other than a *Tyrannosaurus rex*.

Inside the fossil poop, you can see several large bits of dinosaur bone (the black shapes).

This giant piece of fossil poop is the work of a *T. rex*.

Scavenger or Hunter?

Years ago, a few paleontologists wondered if *Tyrannosaurus rex* might have been only a scavenger. They thought that *T. rex* never attacked live prey and only ate animals that were already dead. Those paleontologists were wrong, but they had some good reasons for thinking the way that they did. For one, *T. rex* had a great sense of smell, just like modern turkey vultures do. Turkey vultures are scavengers and use their exceptional sense of smell to find rotting meat across great distances. Also, *T. rex* had teeth and jaws that were able to break bone, just like the teeth and jaws of hyenas. Hyenas are predators that often attack live prey, but they also do a lot of scavenging. The ability to break open bones allows scavenging hyenas to get at meat that is still inside the hollow spaces of a skeleton.

Hyenas have powerful bites that can crush even thick bone.

Scotty chows down on an unfortunate *Edmontosaurus.*

That lets them scrounge up a meal from a dead body, even after the outside had been picked clean by whatever predators did the killing.

But *Tyrannosaurus rex* had plenty of traits that make more sense for a predator to have, like its excellent eyesight and long legs. *T. rex* probably did scavenge when it was lucky enough to find a recently dead animal. After all, few carnivores will turn down a free meal.

However, we now know for sure that *T. rex* did attack live dinosaurs. How can we be so certain? Paleontologists have found tail bones of the duck-billed dinosaur *Edmontosaurus* with *T. rex* teeth still stuck inside of them. The bone around these stuck teeth had started to heal. To create a fossil like that, a *T. rex* must have bitten the duckbill's tail. Then, the lucky duckbill managed to pull away. When it did, it took a tooth with it. Afterwards, the duckbill lived long enough for its tail to start healing. Clearly, the duckbill must have been alive, and not already a dead body, when all of this happened.

T.rex Tooth

This gross-looking mass of bone is actually two tail bones from the duck-billed dinosaur *Edmontosaurus*. Why have the two bones grown into one big lump? Because both were badly damaged while the *Edmontosaurus* was alive. As the two bones healed, they grew into each other. What caused the damage? Still stuck inside the bones is the tooth of a *Tyrannosaurus*.

Dr. Eric Snively
The Tiniest Tyrannosaurus

Scotty may be the biggest *T. rex*, but the Royal Saskatchewan Museum is also home to the very smallest. No one knows much about this tiny *T. rex*. We only have one bone! It's a metatarsal (a limb bone, from between the ankle and the toes). Dr. Eric Snively has studied this little metatarsal carefully. Even though it's much smaller, its shape matches the metatarsals of other *T. rex*. Dr. Snively estimates that from snout to tail tip, the little *T. rex* was only about a metre long. It would have weighed about the same as a house cat. How old was it? Less than one year old. This was a *T. rex* that had only recently hatched from its egg.

Even though it was a hatchling, Dr. Snively thinks the tiny *T. rex* was far from helpless. Hatchling birds that sit in their nests and wait for mom and dad to bring them food usually have limb

Actual Size

This metatarsal belongs to a baby *Tyrannosaurus*.

bones that are a bit soft and not able to support their weight. This means the little birds will fall if they try to stand up. The hatchling *T. rex* metatarsal is solid and seems more than capable of supporting the little dinosaur's weight. It's more like a limb bone from a baby ostrich, chicken or duck. Those baby birds are **precocial**, meaning they hatch ready for action, with legs and feet that are strong enough for walking and even running. Dr. Snively concludes that a hatchling *T. rex* didn't need to hang out in the nest for very long. Instead, it could keep up with its parents, run away from danger and maybe even hunt for small prey on its own.

At ten months old, Scotty was no top predator. It was smaller than a poodle, but it was a swift runner.

Teenage Terrors

As a baby, how quickly did Scotty grow? Much quicker than a baby human grows. By age four, a *Tyrannosaurus rex* would have been as big as a full-grown horse. As most animals grow up, they change in ways other than just getting bigger. When you were a baby, you didn't just look like a short version of how you look today. As a baby, you had a head that was larger compared to the rest of your body, and your arms and legs were much shorter. The study of how animals change as they age is called **ontogeny**.

As a tyrannosaurid aged, it changed in many ways. One of the biggest changes was in the legs. In an adult tyrannosaurid, the leg bones below the knee (the fibula and tibia) were about the same length as the one big leg bone above the knee (the

Teenage Scotty still couldn't safely attack large herbivorous dinosaurs, but young *T. rex* could outrun most animals.

femur). Young tyrannosaurids had lower-leg bones that were much longer than the upper-leg bone. Today, longer lower-leg bones are seen in very fast animals. For this reason, many paleontologists think young long-legged tyrannosaurids were probably faster than the adults.

Which was worse, a fast but small tyrannosaurid teenager or a slower but bigger tyrannosaurid adult? For you and me, it probably wouldn't matter. A teenage tyrannosaurid was still big enough to easily bite us in half, and a big adult was still fast enough to catch us. But the difference was very important to many plant-eating dinosaurs. Some small herbivores could outrun adult tyrannosaurids but not the teenagers.

As a teenager, Scotty had long legs compared to the rest of its body.

Some armoured and horned dinosaurs were too tough and dangerous to have been attacked by anything less than a full-grown tyrannosaurid. This means that the kind of prey a tyrannosaurid could successfully hunt changed as it grew.

TEAM REX:
Dr. Phil Currie
Buried with Children

How did tyrannosaurids hunt? Did they lie in wait behind groves of trees and lunge out in surprise attacks? Did they run down prey in deadly chases? Dr. Phil Currie thinks many tyrannosaurids did both but at different times in their lives. He also thinks they may have hunted together in packs.

In the Gobi Desert of Mongolia and the badlands of Alberta, Canada, Dr. Currie has found skeletons of young tyrannosaurids buried alongside much larger adults. What killed them? Probably a huge flood or other natural disaster. Dr. Currie thinks that all these tyrannosaurids wound up dying together because they had all been living together. The adult tyrannosaurids may have been the young tyrannosaurids' parents. Dr. Currie suspects that young and old tyrannosaurids had different jobs to do when their pack went hunting. With their long legs, the young tyrannosaurids were good at chasing after even the fastest dinosaurs. The big adults had the jaw power to kill just about anything that came within reach. Dr. Currie imagines a tyrannosaurid hunt might have gone like this:

A herd of duckbills grazes on an open plain. Suddenly, seven young tyrannosaurids charge them! The duckbills run, but the young tyrannosaurids are fast and easily keep up. Snapping and snarling, they drive one duckbill away from the herd and towards a low hill. Out from behind that hill rush two big adult tyrannosaurids. The pack's strategy has worked. Chomp! Chomp! In two bites, the duckbill is doomed, and all the tyrannosaurids have a meal.

Some scientists think *T. rex* and other tyrannosaurids hunted in packs. Faster youngsters may have chased prey, while big adults dealt the killing bites.

The Tongue Bone

Did *T. rex* have a long tongue, like many lizards do? Was it forked like a snake's? Tongues are muscles, and muscles don't normally fossilize—they rot away. However, paleontologists are often able to figure out the sizes and shapes of dinosaur muscles by carefully examining the bones that those muscles would have attached to. Giving muscles something hard and firm to pull on is one major reason why animals have bones. Is there a tongue bone? Yes. It's called the **hyoid**. The hyoid is not normally inside the tongue. Instead, it sits at the tongue's base, just in front of the throat and in between the right and left sides of the lower jaw. In most lizards and snakes, the hyoid is big and has a complicated shape. In a chameleon, the hyoid has joints and moving parts that

Actual Size

This is a *T. rex* hyoid. Compared to the skull, the hyoid is small. That means *T. rex* had a small tongue.

help the tongue shoot way out of the throat, capture insects and bring them back into the mouth.

Is the hyoid of *Tyrannosaurus rex* large and complicated? No. It's simple and small. This tells us that *T. rex* did not have the shooting tongue of a chameleon or the forked tongue of a snake. Instead, *T. rex* had a tongue similar to that of a crocodile. It was short—so short that a *T. rex* probably couldn't stick it out past its teeth. That was bad for making silly faces, but it meant *T. rex* was never in danger of biting its own tongue off.

Lizard Lips

Do you have a toy *Tyrannosaurus*? Go look at its mouth. Notice anything missing? Probably, your toy doesn't have any lips. Most toys, pictures and movie special effects show *Tyrannosaurus* as totally lipless. This helps make *Tyrannosaurus* look scarier. After all, lips would cover up some of the big teeth. To be fair, there's reason to think *Tyrannosaurus* didn't have lips. The closest living relatives of *Tyrannosaurus* sure don't. Birds are modern dinosaurs, and they're lipless. Crocodiles and alligators are the next closest relatives of *Tyrannosaurus*, and they also lack lips. However,

Most *T. rex* toys look extra toothy because they lack lips.

Don't let the lips of a Komodo dragon fool you. These big lizards have plenty of teeth.

I think those toys, pictures and movies have got it wrong.

Your lips do many helpful things. They kiss the ones you love, they hold in your food while you chew, they help you slurp through a straw and they also keep your teeth wet. *Tyrannosaurus* probably did not kiss its loved ones (but it might have). It certainly did not drink through a straw. Nor did *Tyrannosaurus* need lips to hold in food while it chewed. *Tyrannosaurus* did not chew at all. It swallowed big mouthfuls whole. But *Tyrannosaurus* did need lips to keep its teeth wet. If teeth dry out, they get brittle and can eventually crack. *Tyrannosaurus* needed healthy teeth for crunching through bone. Birds don't need lips because they have toothless beaks. Crocodiles and alligators aren't worried about their teeth drying out because they live in water.

On a *Tyrannosaurus* skull, just above the teeth, the bones aren't smooth. Instead, there are many small pits. These are the same sorts of pits that, in many other animals, hold lip nerves and little lip muscles. When thinking of the face of *Tyrannosaurus*, don't imagine a lipless mouth, like a crocodile's. Instead, think of big carnivorous lizards, like the modern Komodo dragon. Komodo dragons have sharp and scary teeth, but they also have lips to keep them wet and strong.

Dr. Scott Persons
Big Softy?

When I was a kid I always wanted to pet a *Tyrannosaurus rex*. Now that I am grown up and a paleontologist, I still want to. But what would that feel like? Would a *T. rex* feel soft, hard, cold, warm? Many close relatives of *T. rex* were definitely soft and warm. We have discovered the fossil skeletons of tyrannosauroids, like *Dilong* and *Yutyrannus,* covered with fossil feathers. These coats of fuzzy feathers worked just like the coat of hair on a dog or cat. The feathers helped to hold in body heat and kept the dinosaurs warm.

Did *Tyrannosaurus rex* also have feathers? Yes, I think so . . . but probably only a few. In my research, I helped identify fossil skin

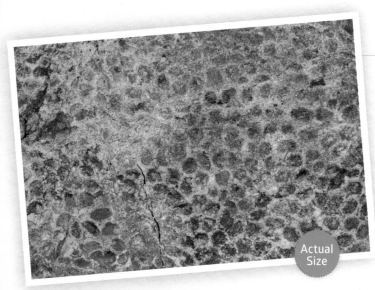

This is the fossil skin of a tyrannosauroid.

Actual Size

Early dinosaur feathers were simple and looked like hair. As feathers evolved, they became more complex and had many stringy branches. Such feathers were still useless for flight, but they helped hold in body heat and kept dinosaurs warm. Eventually, feathers evolved to be stiff, and their branches grew super-small hooks that connected the branches together. This made feathers broad and leaf-shaped. Such leaf-shaped feathers helped one group of dinosaurs glide longer distances when jumping through the treetops. Finally, these dinosaurs evolved true wings and used their feathers to fly.

from *T. rex*. The skin has big scales, not feathery fuzz. How come? Well, *T. rex* was very large, even compared to other tyrannosauroids, and it lived in a warm environment. Think about modern mammals that are very large and live where it's hot. Think about elephants, rhinos and hippos. Those big mammals don't have much hair. Don't they get cold? No, their big bodies produce so much heat and their environments are so warm that it's actually a bigger challenge to stay cool. That's why they have so little hair. The same was probably true of *T. rex*. If you could reach out and pet a *T. rex*, most of its body would feel rough and scaly, but still warm.

A newly hatched *T. rex* might have needed a coat of fuzzy feathers to keep it warm.

A Warm-Blooded Killer

Scientists used to think that *Tyrannosaurus* was cold-blooded or **ectothermic**. Ectothermic animals don't produce their own body heat. Instead, they warm themselves up by lying in the sun or on top of hot rocks that have already been warmed by the sun. Ectothermic animals also can't cool themselves down. Instead, they must leave any place that has gotten too hot and go someplace that is cooler, like a nice spot in the shade or a cool burrow. Modern ectothermic animals include salamanders, frogs, lizards, turtles and crocodiles. Warm-blooded or **endothermic** animals can produce their own body heat. Their bodies do this by burning energy. Endotherms can also cool themselves off by sweating or panting. We humans are endothermic animals. So are birds, wombats, cats, dogs and other mammals.

Cold weather doesn't slow down this red squirrel. The little endotherm burns energy to keep itself warmer than the snowy world around it.

Compared to us, ectothermic animals have it easier in several ways. Not having to burn energy to stay warm

means a turtle doesn't have to find as much food to eat. Not sweating or panting to stay cool also means a lizard doesn't waste water. But being endothermic has advantages too. Being able to keep ourselves warm means we can live in places that are very cold. It also means we can stay active even when the weather turns cool. Being able to keep ourselves cool by sweating means that we can exercise for a long time, without having to stop and rest in a shady place. It also means we can stay out in the sun longer, even when the weather turns hot. Staying at our ideal temperature and eating much more also means that endothermic animals grow more quickly.

As an ectotherm, this lizard must bask in the sun to warm up.

Feeling a bit too hot, the lizard must cool off in the shade.

Today, paleontologists are pretty sure dinosaurs were endothermic. We can tell because many small dinosaurs had coats of feathers to hold in their body heat. We also know dinosaurs grew much faster than the ectothermic crocodiles and turtles that lived at the same time.

That makes Scotty a much scarier creature. As an endotherm, *Tyrannosaurus* could hunt whether the temperature was hot or cold. It could hunt without needing to rest in the sun or in the shade. Scariest of all, as an endothermic animal that burned energy to keep warm, Scotty would have needed to eat a lot of meat and would have gotten hungrier much faster.

Chapter 4

THE WORLD OF SCOTTY

Where and When

The first dinosaurs evolved roughly 235 million years ago. The Age of Dinosaurs lasted for over 160 million years, but *Tyrannosaurus rex* was "king of the dinosaurs" for only about two million years. As time went on, many different dinosaur species evolved and many species went extinct. This means different kinds of dinosaurs lived at different times. Across the world, different dinosaur fossils have been found on every continent. So, different kinds of dinosaurs also evolved to live in different kinds of environments. *T. rex* only lived in what is today western North America and only at the very end of the **Cretaceous Period** (the chunk of time

Glacialisaurus: Antarctica, Early Jurassic, 185 million years ago

Stegosaurus: North America, Late Jurassic, 150 million years ago

Spinosaurus: Africa, Late Cretaceous, 95 million years ago between 145 and 65.5 million years ago). Scotty never got the chance to see (or eat) most dinosaur species.

Kingdom by the Sea

During the Age of Dinosaurs, the earth's climate was very different. Volcanic gasses thickened the **atmosphere**. These gasses held in extra heat, which kept the planet much warmer than it is today. It was so warm that there were no ice caps at the North or South Pole. This made ocean levels higher. In North America, some of this extra water flooded the continent. A long, shallow seaway filled the lowlands in the middle of North America. We call this body of water the **Western Interior Seaway**. During the time of *Tyrannosaurus*, the Western Interior Seaway teemed with fish and marine reptiles. Scotty lived near the western shore of this narrow sea.

Sixty-six million years ago, the world was hot and sea levels were high.

Muttaburrasaurus:
Australia, Early Cretaceous, 110 million years ago

Amargasaurus:
South America, Early Cretaceous, 125 million years ago

T. rex lived only in North America, 66 million years ago. That means most dinosaurs (like all of these) never saw a *T. rex*.

TEAM REX:
Dr. Hallie Street
Sea Monster

Sixty-six million years ago, *Tyran-nosaurus* wasn't the only gigantic carnivore on the hunt. Giant marine reptiles lived in the Western Interior Seaway. Dr. Hallie Street studies one of the largest and most fearsome of these ancient sea monsters—**mosasaurs**. Mosasaurs were a kind of lizard that evolved to live in the water. Mosasaurs had webbed feet and strong tails tipped with a large, fleshy fin.

The jaws of a mosasaur were long, like a crocodile's. Their teeth were usually long, sharp and curved back towards the throat. These backwards-curving teeth made it hard for a big fish, shark, or other

Extra Teeth

This is the skull of a mosasaur. Look closely and you can see an extra set of teeth at the back of the mouth.

This is the flipper of a mosasaur uncovered in the badlands of Saskatchewan.

marine reptile to pull itself out of a mosasaur's mouth. To hold on to especially slippery seafood, the mouth of a mosasaur had two extra rows of teeth. These were the **palatal teeth**, and they grew on the roof of the mouth.

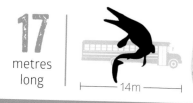

MOSASAURUS
(not a dinosaur)
PRONUNCIATION: MO-sa-SAWR-us

MEANING: Meuse River lizard
AGE: Late Cretaceous, 70–66 million years ago
HABITAT: Shallow seaways
DIET: Large sea creatures

17 metres long

14m

91

Up in the Sky

Pterosaurs were flying reptiles that lived during the Age of Dinosaurs. They had long arms and one really long finger. A pterosaur's wing was formed by thick skin stretched between its legs, body, arms and the long finger of each hand. Many pterosaurs were small (no bigger than a modern seagull) but some were true giants of the sky. The largest pterosaurs had wingspans of over ten metres. They were the largest animals ever to fly.

Pterosaurs are often mistakenly called the "flying dinosaurs." Although pterosaurs are closely related to dinosaurs, they aren't true dinosaurs. However, Scotty's world was filled with many flying creatures that *were* dinosaurs: birds. Tens of millions of years earlier, birds had evolved from small carnivorous dinosaurs. By the time of *Tyrannosaurus*, there were many different species of birds. Some hunted for seeds and nuts in the trees, some caught fish in the sea and many ate the insects that also fluttered and flew through the prehistoric skies.

QUETZALCOATLUS
(not a dinosaur)

PRONUNCIATION: KET-zal-koh-at-lus

MEANING: Of the feathered serpent god Quetzalcoatl

AGE: Late Cretaceous, 68–66 million years ago

HABITAT: Savannahs

DIET: Unknown

11 metre wingspan

├─── 14m ───┤

TEAM REX:
Dr. Ryan McKellar
Nuggets of Wisdom

Dr. Ryan McKellar is an invertebrate paleontologist. That means he studies prehistoric animals that did not have backbones. That's not an easy job. Most animals that don't have backbones also don't have limb bones, skull bones or any bones at all. Not having a skeleton makes it difficult for invertebrates to leave any kind of fossil remains behind. Some invertebrates, like snails and clams, do have hard shells, and those shells often fossilize. But Dr. McKellar doesn't study snails or clams. He mostly works on insects.

Insect fossils are rare. To find them, Dr. McKellar relies on another kind of fossil: **amber**. Amber is fossilized tree **resin**. Trees make resin for many reasons, but one reason is to stick to and permanently hold on to insects that are trying to eat the tree. Dr. McKellar collects nuggets of amber. He looks for insects that might

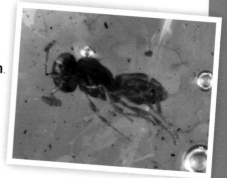

have gotten stuck in the resin and wound up being fossilized within it. Thanks to amber, we know that Scotty's world was abuzz with many kinds of insects, including wasps, beetles, ants and flies.

This fossil wasp is preserved inside amber.

TEAM REX:
Dr. Emily Bamforth
Plant Life

Dinosaur bones were not the only fossils discovered at the Scotty quarry. While chiselling through the hard rock, paleontologists found the fossil shells of prehistoric clams and the fossilized leaves of many different kinds of trees. Dr. Emily Bamforth has studied these leaves and worked hard to identify what kinds of trees they came from. She learned that Scotty's home was very different from

Paleontologists collected these leaf fossils at the Scotty quarry. You can see that the leaves belong to many different kinds of plants.

Scotty lived in a warm, forested environment. It was filled not just with dinosaurs, but with little mammals, turtles, crocodiles, frogs and lots of insects.

Today, cypress forests can still be found. They grow in warm and wet environments.

the Saskatchewan of today. There were no dry badlands or snowy prairies. Scotty's world was wet, hot and lush. Dr. Bamforth's leaves came from palm, fig and cypress trees. These are plants that need moist, warm weather for most of the year. Many of the other plant fossils were from low-growing plants, like ferns and cycads (which look like pineapples).

Creatures Great and Small

Pterosaurs, dinosaurs and mosasaurs are all animals that lived in Scotty's world but have now gone extinct. Keep in mind, however, that many of the other animals that lived alongside Scotty were very similar to ones that are still alive today. For example, there were turtles, snakes, crocodiles, frogs, salamanders, spiders and dragonflies.

There were also mammals. Today, many mammals are large animals, but during the Age of Dinosaurs, they were all small. None even reached the size of a cocker spaniel, and most were the size of mice. Being small made it easier to hide from carnivorous dinosaurs. Most of the mammals that lived at the same time as Scotty hunted insects or ate seeds. Many of these little mammals were good climbers. To find their food and also stay hidden from dinosaurs, most of them moved under the cover of darkness. They were nocturnal, meaning they were active mainly at night.

The modern opossum is a mammal similar to many that lived at the same time as Scotty. Opossums like to hide during the day and only come out at night.

TEAM REX:
Dr. Robert Bakker
A *Tyrannosaurus* Grows Up

Like you and me, Dr. Robert Bakker likes to imagine what it would be like to be a *T. rex*. So, suppose you're a little *Tyrannosaurus*. You have just hatched from your egg. You shake off a bit of shell that is still sitting on your face, and you take your first look at the world around you. It's a scary place. Hiding behind the trees and bushes could be raptors, crocodiles or some big herbivorous dinosaur that would be happy to stomp on a baby predator. Would you have to survive all that on your own? Or, when you take your first peek at the world, would the friendly face of your mother be there to greet and guide you? Dr. Bakker thinks she would be.

Paleontologists have not yet found the eggs or nest of a *Tyrannosaurus*. We have no way to tell for sure if *Tyrannosaurus* was a good parent. Instead, Dr. Bakker has looked at relatives of *Tyrannosaurus*. Crocodiles and alligators are their close living relatives, and birds are living dinosaurs. Most birds are very good parents. Mother birds (and often fathers, too) do their best to protect their chicks. Many bring their chicks food until the chicks are big enough to find it themselves. Crocodiles and alligators are also good moms. A mother alligator will fiercely guard her nest. When the little gators hatch, the mother will delicately carry them in her mouth to water. Once they're in the water, their mother will stick around to keep away other predators.

Dr. Bakker has also studied other kinds of big carnivorous dinosaurs, like *Allosaurus*. He has discovered the bones of huge herbivorous dinosaurs that have been munched on by both baby and adult *Allosaurus*. The babies were far too small to have attacked such big prey. Dr. Bakker reasons that the adult *Allosaurus* must have been the ones that did the attacking. Then, the adults brought the food to their babies. If at least one kind of big carnivorous dinosaur was a good parent, it's likely that many others—including *Tyrannosaurus*—were as well.

Would Scotty have been a good parent? Many birds and crocodilians are.

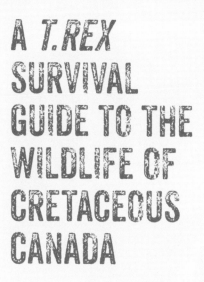

A *T. REX* SURVIVAL GUIDE TO THE WILDLIFE OF CRETACEOUS CANADA

WARNING! DINOSAURS AHEAD!

As the many wounds on Scotty's skeleton show, a *Tyrannosaurus* had a tough life. The typical *Tyrannosaurus* did not live very long. A *Tyrannosaurus* was a powerful predator, but it could not just charge in, mouth open, and attack whatever it wanted. The prehistoric world of *Tyrannosaurus* was filled with other scary carnivores and many well-armed herbivores. To survive, a *Tyrannosaurus* needed to know the best way to hunt each of the different kinds of dinosaurs that shared its world. As the longest-lived *Tyrannosaurus*, Scotty was the ultimate survivor.

ACHERORAPTOR

PRONUNCIATION: ah-SHEH-ro-RAP-tor

MEANING: Underworld thief

DIET: Small and medium-sized animals (including mammals, lizards, pterosaurs and other dinosaurs)

HOW TO ATTACK: Raptors can turn quickly and they're excellent jumpers, but their skeletons aren't particularly strong and they have no armour. One bite will do it.

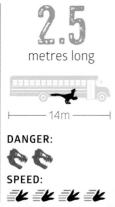

2.5 metres long

├─ 14m ─┤

DANGER:

SPEED:

Super Slasher

Acheroraptor was a **deinonychosaur** or "raptor" dinosaur.
Deinonychosaurs were predatory dinosaurs related to
tyrannosauroids and very closely related to birds.
Like most predatory dinosaurs, deinonychosaurs had strong jaws filled with sharp teeth, and
fingers and toes tipped with sharp claws. Unlike
other predatory dinosaurs, deinonychosaurs had
one extremely large claw on their biggest toe.
This claw was strongly curved and was carried in
a raised position. Having the claw raised meant it
did not scratch the ground as it walked. That kept
the claw sharp. A kick from a deinonychosaur foot
would leave a long and deep cut.

Deinonychosaurs
had scary feet.
The inside toe was
raised and armed
with a hooked claw.

Deinonychosaurs were excellent tree climbers. Paleontologists
know from fossil footprints that some deinonychosaurs travelled
in packs and walked side by side. Fossilized feathers show that deinonychosaurs had a covering of feathers across their bodies and
many deinonychosaurs had long feathers on their arms and tails.

Raptor Snack

Many raptor dinosaurs were fast, but most were slower than a
young tyrannosaurid. Did raptor dinosaurs, like *Acheroraptor*, ever get eaten by *Tyrannosaurus*? Yep.
We know that for sure, thanks to the discovery of a raptor skeleton inside the rib cage of
a tyrannosaurid—right where the stomach
would have been. That poor raptor
must have been the tyrannosaurid's last meal.

Rex vs. Rex

Just because two animals are the same species doesn't mean they'll get along. Maybe *T. rex* lived in packs, and probably *T. rex* was a good parent. But when two *T. rex* from different packs or different families met, there could be trouble! Remember, in nature, there's usually not enough of everything to go around. Today, animals of the same species often fight each other over the best hunting territory, or the best nesting spot, or just because one wants to eat the other. Often, full-grown adults will try very hard to eat the babies of other members of the same species. Why? Because those babies could grow up to be serious competition.

Skeletons with bite marks show that tyrannosauroids were not always friendly towards other tyrannosauroids—even members of the same species.

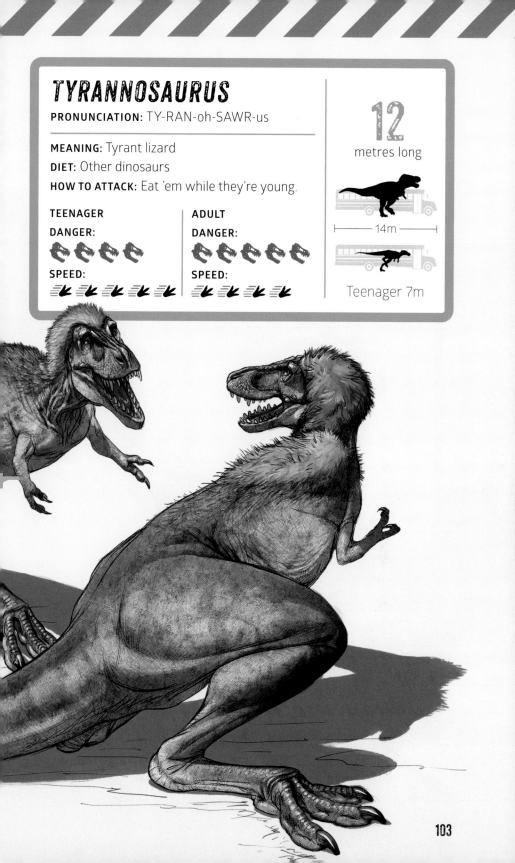

TYRANNOSAURUS

PRONUNCIATION: TY-RAN-oh-SAWR-us

MEANING: Tyrant lizard

DIET: Other dinosaurs

HOW TO ATTACK: Eat 'em while they're young.

TEENAGER
DANGER:

SPEED:

ADULT
DANGER:

SPEED:

12 metres long

14m

Teenager 7m

Fast Food

Struthiomimus was a relative of *Tyrannosaurus* and the raptor dinosaurs, but it had evolved to be mostly herbivorous. With no teeth, horns or armour, *Struthiomimus* was a favourite prey of *Tyrannosaurus* ... when *T. rex* could catch it. *Struthiomimus* was among the very fastest

STRUTHIOMIMUS

PRONUNCIATION:
stru-THEE-oh-MY-mus

MEANING: Ostrich mimic

DIET: Plants

HOW TO ATTACK: Don't let it get a head start. Try to get in close and take it by surprise.

DANGER:

SPEED:

4.5 metres long

|— 14m —|

of all known dinosaurs. It had long leg bones and powerful leg muscles. As an adult, *Tyrannosaurus* was too slow to catch a *Struthiomimus*, unless it took the speedy dinosaur by surprise. A young *Tyrannosaurus* could almost match *Struthiomimus* in speed. Like modern cheetahs and gazelles, young *Tyrannosaurus* and *Struthiomimus* must have taken part in many high-speed chases.

Trike Force

Scotty never met
a more
dangerous herb-
ivorous dinosaur
than a healthy adult
Triceratops. The horned
dinosaur was bigger than an
elephant and heavily
armed. The horns over
the eyes were each
more than a metre
long. These were the
major horns that
a *Tyrannosaurus*
needed to watch out
for, but there was
also a smaller horn
on the end of the snout. If
the *Triceratops* succeeded in
striking head-on, the nose horn could also stab
a *Tyrannosaurus*. The name "three-horned face"
comes from these three main horns, but the face
of *Triceratops* actually had a lot more than three
horns. The shield at the back of a *Triceratops* skull is
called a "frill." The frill was made of thick bone and
small horns lined its edge. This made the frill dangerous to bite on. *Triceratops* also had a pair of jugal
horns just behind its cheeks. These pointed down
to protect the side of the face.

In a battle, could a *Triceratops* really best a big
Tyrannosaurus like Scotty? Absolutely. If the

TRICERATOPS

PRONUNCIATION: TRY-sair-a-TOPS

MEANING: Three-horned face

DIET: Plants

HOW TO ATTACK: Surprise from behind (never attack head-on!)

DANGER: 🦖🦖🦖🦖🦖 **SPEED:** 🐾🐾

10

metres long

|— 14m —|

Triceratops managed to stab the *T. rex* deeply with one of its bigger horns, that would be it. However, to avoid being eaten, herbivores don't necessarily have to be able to kill their predators. They just need to be so dangerous that the predators decide it's better to wait and attack something else. Unless the *Triceratops* was sick, injured or very young, it would have been risky to attack. Scotty didn't live to be the biggest and oldest *Tyrannosaurus* by taking unnecessary risks.

Big-Headed Relatives

Torosaurus is a very close relative of *Triceratops*. In fact, some paleontologists think that *Torosaurus* might be just another species of *Triceratops*. What makes them different? When fully grown, a *Torosaurus* had a much taller frill. The frill of *Torosaurus* is so long that it gave *Torosaurus* the longest skull of any land animal ever! But, while *Triceratops* had a frill made of thick bone and lined with spiky horns, the frill of *Torosaurus* was hornless and made of much thinner bone. Although *Torosaurus* had a larger frill, the thin bone made it more delicate. Such a frill may have been less useful as a shield, but it was great for a different job. Like the head crests of many birds, the big frill of *Torosaurus* would have been an eye-catching display. Having such a huge frill was like carrying around its own billboard advertisement. The frill was used to attract a mate and may have been waved about during courtship dances.

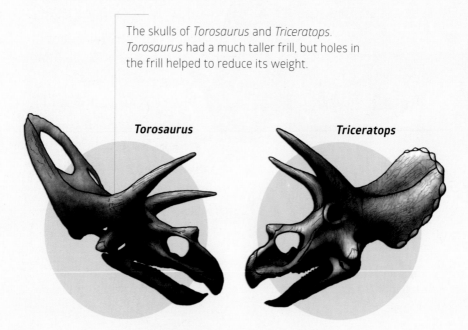

The skulls of *Torosaurus* and *Triceratops*. *Torosaurus* had a much taller frill, but holes in the frill helped to reduce its weight.

Torosaurus

Triceratops

TOROSAURUS

PRONUNCIATION: TOR-oh-SOR-us

MEANING: Bull lizard

DIET: Plants

HOW TO ATTACK: These dinosaurs don't travel in large herds, but they can live in small family groups. If you spot a young one, make sure there's not a parent nearby.

DANGER: 🦖🦖🦖🦖🦖 **SPEED:** 🐾🐾

10
metres long

14m

Hide and Seek

About the size of a modern sheep, *Leptoceratops* was a small relative of *Triceratops* and *Torosaurus*. Like its bigger relations, *Leptoceratops* had a neck frill and a parrot-like beak, but it didn't have long horns. Naturally, a *Leptoceratops* would have been much safer prey to attack than its big-horned relatives. But *Leptoceratops* was probably not an easy dinosaur to find. Being small, *Leptoceratops* could hide in brush, in burrows or in the water. The broad tail and big feet of *Leptoceratops* probably made it a good swimmer.

LEPTOCERATOPS

PRONUNCIATION:
lep-TOH-sair-a-TOPS

MEANING: Little-horned face

DIET: Plants

HOW TO ATTACK: Keep your eyes on the prize, and make sure it doesn't get to cover.

DANGER:  SPEED:

2 metres long

6m

Hard Headed

Pachycephalosaurus was a distant relative of horned dinosaurs like *Triceratops*. It had a thick, bony dome on the top of its head. This dome was surrounded by many small horns. *Pachycephalosaurus* wasn't very fast, but it was strong for its size. Like a ram or a bighorn sheep, a *Pachycephalosaurus* likely used its armoured skull to head-butt other *Pachycephalosaurus*. Such head-to-head fights could have been over territory, rank within a herd or the chance to mate. An adult *Tyrannosaurus* could have made an easy meal of a *Pachycephalosaurus*, but a young *Tyrannosaurus* would have been in serious trouble if it got hit with a headlong battering-ram charge.

PACHYCEPHALOSAURUS

PRONUNCIATION: pac-KEY-sef-a-lo-SAWR-us

MEANING: Thick-headed lizard

DIET: Plants (possibly some small animals)

HOW TO ATTACK: Don't bite the head, or you'll break a tooth.

DANGER: **SPEED:**

4.5
metres long

├─── 14m ───┤

Safety in Numbers

The enormous duck-billed dinosaur *Edmontosaurus* was one of the most common herbivorous dinosaurs in Scotty's world. At more than three tons, an *Edmontosaurus* made for a grand feast. *Edmontosaurus* was slower than *Tyrannosaurus* and it had no scary weapons. Still, *Edmontosaurus* was no easy meal. The duckbill may have been a slower runner, but it had better endurance. This meant it could outrun a *Tyrannosaurus* over a long distance. To stay alive, *Edmontosaurus* needed to make sure a *Tyrannosaurus* never snuck in too close. *Edmontosaurus* had excellent eyesight and hearing. It also had a neck that could easily swing its head around to scan for danger in all directions. Most importantly, an *Edmontosaurus* usually had help. This dinosaur lived in large herds. Being part of a big herd meant there were always many other watchful eyes and listening ears around you, all of them working together to notice any stalking *Tyrannosaurus*.

Power Muncher

Some dinosaurs had weird faces. The long snouts and big beaks of *Edmontosaurus* and its relatives gave the group its nickname: the "duck-billed" dinosaurs. The bill of *Edmontosaurus* wasn't really like a duck's, and the dinosaur sure didn't eat like one. For starters, the edge of the big beak was sharp. That made it good at nipping and slicing off large mouthfuls of plants. Behind the beak, *Edmontosaurus* had many rows of teeth. These teeth were small, but they all fit together tightly. All these teeth formed large surfaces that were used to grind and chew up plants.

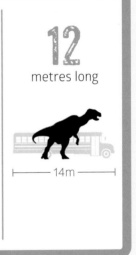

EDMONTOSAURUS

PRONUNCIATION:
ed-MON-toh-SAWR-us

MEANING: Lizard from the Edmonton Formation

DIET: Plants

HOW TO ATTACK: Look for sick, very old or very young members of the herd.

DANGER:

SPEED:

12
metres long

├─── 14m ───┤

The skull of *Edmontosaurus* is a shrub's worst nightmare. The big beak at the front is for slicing off leaves and shoots. The rows of teeth at the back are for grinding.

Body Armour

It's often said (and you may have read in other books) that *Ankylosaurus* was a dinosaur built like a turtle. But that's not really true. Turtles have a smooth, hard shell as armour. *Ankylosaurus* had a head, neck, back, legs and tail covered with bony plates. Like the shell of a turtle, these armour plates were coated by keratin—the same stuff that covers most animal claws and horns (including Scotty's). Keratin is tough stuff, and it made the armour of *Ankylosaurus* stronger. But this dinosaur was no turtle, and its armour was far from smooth.

In a way, *Ankylosaurus* was more like a porcupine or a hedgehog. Many of its bony plates had raised peaks and strong ridges. The keratin covering the plates turned the raised peaks into spikes and the strong ridges into sharp edges. A

ANKYLOSAURUS

PRONUNCIATION: AN-ky-low-SAWR-us

MEANING: Fused lizard

DIET: Low-growing plants

HOW TO ATTACK: There's no armour on the belly. Try to flip it, and avoid the tail!

DANGER: 🦖🦖🦖🦖🦖   **SPEED:** 🦶

9 metres long

├── 14m ──┤

Tyrannosaurus would not have wanted to step or jump onto the back of an *Ankylosaurus*. It would have cut its own foot! *Ankylosaurus* could also use its many spikes and sharp edges as weapons. A good shove from the side by an *Ankylosaurus* would have cut and stabbed a *Tyrannosaurus* in many places.

The Business End

The most dangerous part of an *Ankylosaurus* was its tail. Along the sides of the tail were many small armoured spikes. At the very end of the tail, several large pieces of armour grew together to form a single heavy mass. The armour that formed this mass was covered in keratin and had sharp edges. Enormous tail muscles at the hips could swing

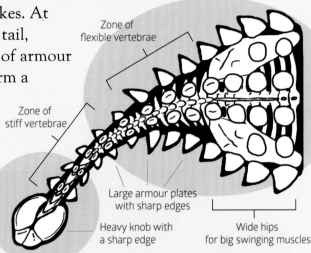

Zone of
flexible vertebrae

Zone of
stiff vertebrae

Large armour plates
with sharp edges

Heavy knob with
a sharp edge

Wide hips
for big swinging muscles

the tail like a battle-axe. The tail of *Ankylosaurus* had the power to smash and hack the leg muscles and bones of any *Tyrannosaurus* that didn't get out of the way.

This is an armoured plate from the back of an ankylosaur. Have a look at the sharp ridge.

THE NEXT BIG FIND

Unbreakable Record?

Was Scotty the biggest *Tyrannosaurus* that ever lived? Almost certainly not. As a species, *Tyrannosaurus rex* was around for over two million years. Fossils of *Tyrannosaurus* have been found across western North America, from Canada to Mexico. In all that time and all that space, there must have been many millions of them. So

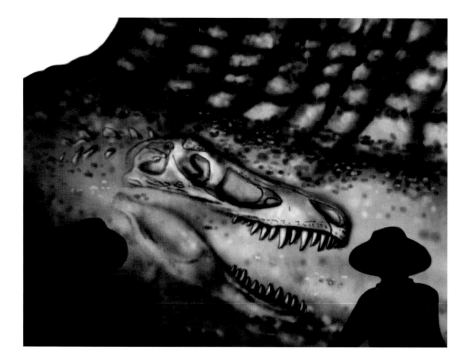

far, paleontologists have only found about fifty skeletons. I'm sure that bigger individuals did live and that the skeletons of at least a few of those bigger individuals were also fossilized. Right now, in some corner of the badlands, the bones of an even bigger *Tyrannosaurus* are waiting to be discovered. Who is going to find them?

The Unsolved

The research on Scotty isn't over, and the research on *Tyrannosaurus rex* has only just begun. There's still a great deal we don't know. One big unanswered question is why Scotty died. The skeleton shows no large wounds that had not already healed. Maybe Scotty was killed in a fight with another dinosaur, and the attack that killed Scotty just didn't break any bones. Maybe Scotty died from a disease, maybe it ate or drank something that was poisonous, maybe it drowned in a flood or was struck by lightning. We may never know. Then again, maybe someday we will. I haven't been able to figure out how Scotty died. But someone else might. Maybe another scientist will think of a new method that lets us test dinosaur bones for certain diseases or poisons. Then, we could discover that Scotty died from sickness or because it drank some bad swamp water.

Today, there are more people studying dinosaurs than ever before. With more paleontologists comes more research and more new ideas. There are many other unsolved mysteries surrounding *T. rex*. I don't know what colour *T. rex* was, or how to tell whether a skeleton is male or female, or if both mother and father *T. rex* cared for their young. However, I think all of these mysteries can be solved, and I bet they will be. I'd like it if some of these mysteries wound up being solved by someone who has read this book.

GLOSSARY

Bold within a glossary definition means the word is also defined in the glossary.

Air scribe: a tool used by **preparators** to break up and remove small amounts of very hard rock that cling to **fossils**. Air scribes work like miniature jack-hammers and are powered by bursts of air squeezed through a tube. They're powerful but can damage fossils, so they must be used carefully.

Amber: fossilized tree **resin**. Amber often contains the **fossils** of insects and other living things that got stuck in the resin before it hardened. Amber is also a gemstone.

Atmosphere: the gas that surrounds a planet.

Badlands: a dry, hilly environment with few plants. In badlands, **erosion** has carved many small canyons and gullies through the hillsides. These eroded hillsides can have many exposed rock layers and often **fossils**.

Binomial: the two-part scientific name given to every **species**. A binomial begins with the **genus** name and ends with the **specific epithet**. In the binomial name *Tyrannosaurus rex*, "*Tyrannosaurus*" is the genus name and "*rex*" is the specific epithet.

Body fossil: the fossilized remains of a body part from a prehistoric living thing. Body fossils include fossil bones, feathers, skin and petrified wood.

Bone histology: the study of the inside of a bone. Usually a histological study starts by taking a small sample of a bone and grinding it down until it's so thin that light can shine through it. Then, the thin sample is placed under a microscope. Bone histology can tell **paleontologists** important information about how the bones of an animal grew.

Camouflage: colours, patterns and body shapes that help an animal blend in with its surroundings.

Carnivorous: meat-eating.

Casts: copies of **fossils** made from moulds of original fossils. Casts aren't sculptures. They show a fossil's true shape and size. Often, casts are made of a lightweight material, so that they're easier and safer to display than the original fossil.

Coprolite: fossilized poop.

Cranial cavity: the hollow space inside the skull that contains the brain.

Cretaceous Period: the chunk of time between 145 and 65.5 million years ago.

Deinonychosaur: a kind of **carnivorous** dinosaur with a large, sharp and strongly curved claw on the biggest toe of each foot. Deinonychosaurs are also known as "raptor dinosaurs." They're closely related to birds, and their bodies were covered in feathers. Most deinonychosaurs were small (about the size of modern foxes and wolves), but some grew to over seven metres in length.

Depth perception: the ability to look at an object and judge how far away it is.

Disarticulated: when a skeleton's bones are no longer attached to each other as they were in life. As a dead body rots, the soft muscles and **ligaments** that hold the bones together disappear. If the skeleton has not been buried before this happens, the bones will come apart.

Ectothermic: being unable to heat and cool your own body through burning energy, sweating or panting. Ectothermic animals must instead warm themselves by basking in the sun, and cool themselves by sheltering in the shade.

Endothermic: being able to heat and cool your own body by burning energy and by sweating or panting.

Erosion: the process of rocks or soil wearing down. Erosion is usually very slow, but sometimes it can be caused suddenly by powerful forces, like floods or volcanic eruptions.

Evolution: the process of **species** accumulating new characteristics over time and of one species gradually changing into a new one.

Evolutionary relationships: the history of change between two or more **species**. Two species are closely related if they haven't changed much since they first split from a shared ancestor.

Excavating: digging up **fossils**. Excavating a large fossil usually involves using big tools, like shovels and pickaxes, to dig around the fossil. **Paleontologists** also use very small tools, like brushes and hand picks, to dig close to it.

Excavators: people who dig up **fossils** in the field.

Femur: the large leg bone between the hip and knee.

Fossil: a natural object from the past that tells us about prehistoric life. Often, fossils are bones, teeth and other hard parts of an animal's body. Most fossils have lasted for millions of years because they were buried safely underground.

Gastralia: small bones that ran along the underbelly of many **carnivorous** dinosaurs. They're often called "belly ribs." Gastralia are movable and help animals take deep breaths. Modern crocodiles also have gastralia.

Genus: a group of closely related living things that may include different **species**. For example, the genus *Triceratops* includes two known species: *Triceratops horridus* and *Triceratops prorsus*. Members of the same genus usually look very similar and play similar roles in their environments. No two genera have the same name.

Herbivorous: plant-eating.

Hyoid: a bone at the start of the neck that tongue muscles attach to.

Inheritance: The passing on of **traits** from parents to their babies. Because of inheritance, young tend to be similar to their parents.

Jugal horn: a small horn positioned over the cheek.

Keratin: a tough material that covers the outside of claws, horns and beaks. Feathers, hair and scales are also made of keratin.

Ligament: a band of tough flesh that connects and holds two bones together.

Mammals: animals that produce milk, have a constant body temperature and usually have hair. Some examples of modern mammals are humans, dogs, whales, rodents and kangaroos.

Mosasaurs: a group of prehistoric marine lizards with flippers and tail fins.

Olfactory bulb: the part of the brain that makes sense of smell.

Ontogeny: the study of how a creature changes as it grows older.

Palatal teeth: a second set of teeth on the roof of the mouth.

Paleoartist: an artist who illustrates the prehistoric world and prehistoric life.

Paleontologist: a scientist who studies fossils and prehistoric life.

Parasites: harmful living things that attach themselves to other living things.

Pathologies: damage from injury or sickness.

Pelvis: the bones of the hip.

Plaster jacket: a protective covering of cloth and hardened plaster that is wrapped around a **fossil** to protect it. Plaster jackets are used to keep fossils safe while they're transported out of the field.

Postorbital boss: a large, lumpy horn just behind and above the eye.

Precocial: able to walk and move about right after hatching or birth.

Preparators: people who clean **fossils** after they have been **excavated** and transported from the field.

Pterosaurs: a group of flying reptiles closely related to dinosaurs. Pterosaurs had wings made of skin stretched from their legs and bodies to one very long finger on each hand.

Quarry: a large dig site where many **fossils** have been found.

Resin: a sticky goo made by many plants. Resin helps plants heal by filling in broken or damaged parts of their woody stems or trunks. Resin also helps plants defend themselves from **herbivores** that are trying to eat them. Tiny herbivores, like insects, may become trapped in sticky resin. Larger herbivores usually don't like the taste or feel of resin stuck in their mouths. Fossilized resin is called **amber.**

Sandstone: rock formed from sand grains that are cemented together. Sandstones often form in environments that were once beaches, rivers or deserts.

Scavengers: carnivores that eat already-dead animals they find, rather than attacking or killing prey.

Scientific publication: a printed or online collection of reports that share research results. Many scientists review and double-check the research in scientific publications to help make sure it's accurate.

Sexual dimorphism: physical differences (other than differences in the sexual organs) between male and female members of the same **species**. Often, males will have larger and more complicated display features and/or brighter colours than females. Males use these features to attract females.

Species: a specific kind of animal, plant or other living thing. Members of the same species can breed with each other, usually look very similar to each other and fill the same roles in their environment.

Specific epithet: the second part of a species' scientific name. For example, in the scientific name *Tyrannosaurus rex*, "*rex*" is the specific epithet.

Stratigraphy: the study of how and when different layers of rocks formed and how they erode away. Stratigraphy also maps rock layers across the world and tries to identify similar layers in different places.

Taphonomy: the scientific study of what happens to the body of a prehistoric animal after death. Taphonomic subjects include how skeletons become **disarticulated**, how bones are buried, how **fossils** form, how fossils are squashed by the weight of rock layers that build up on top of them and how fossils erode.

Trace fossil: a **fossil** that records the activity of prehistoric life. Trace fossils include fossil footprints, **coprolites**, burrows and nests.

Trait: a characteristic of a **species**. Traits may be physical, like skin colour or the shape of a body part. They may also be a way of living, like burrowing, climbing or being nervous.

Tyrannosaurids: a group of **carnivorous** dinosaurs. Tyrannosaurids had large skulls, thick teeth and small arms.

Tyrannosauroids: a group of **carnivorous** dinosaurs that includes **tyrannosaurids**. Early tyrannosauroids were small and had long arms with three fingers. All tyrannosauroids had stiff tails, large hip bones and long legs.

Tyrannosaurus: a **genus** in the **tyrannosaurid** group. Currently, only one **species** of *Tyrannosaurus* is known: *Tyrannosaurus rex*. At thirteen metres long, *Tyrannosaurus* was the biggest known tyrannosaurid. It was also among the very last tyrannosaurids alive.

Vertebra: a bone from the neck, back or tail. Vertebrae string together to form the spinal column.

Western Interior Seaway: a shallow sea that covered much of the middle of North America during the **Cretaceous Period**.

INDEX

About the Authors

DR. W. SCOTT PERSONS IV is a paleontologist and professor at the College of Charleston and the Mace Brown Museum of Natural History. He has taken part in fossil-hunting expeditions throughout the badlands of the American West, the Gobi Desert of Mongolia, the canyons of Tanzania's Olduvai Gorge, the pampas of Argentina and the volcanic ash beds of Northern China. His work has been featured on the National Geographic and Discovery channels and in *Smithsonian* and *Discover* magazines. He lives in Charleston, South Carolina.

BETH ZAIKEN is an artist and illustrator specializing in natural science communication. She has over a decade of experience creating large-scale murals, dioramas and reconstructions of modern and prehistoric animals in both traditional and digital media. She is a principal artist and the lead muralist for Blue Rhino Studio and her work can be seen in such institutions as the Panama Biomuseo, the Sheikh Abdullah Al-Salem Cultural Centre in Kuwait, the Royal Alberta Museum, the Royal Saskatchewan Museum, Chicago's Field Museum, Ancient Ozarks Natural History Museum, the San Diego Zoo, the New York State Museum and the Minnesota Zoo. Her work has also appeared in National Park Service publications. She lives in Minneapolis, Minnesota.